Palgrave Studies in Institutions, Economics and Law

Law and Economics is an interdisciplinary field of research that has emerged in recent decades, with research output increasing dramatically and academic programmes in law and economics multiplying. Increasingly, legal cases have an economic dimension and economic matters depend on rules and regulations. Increasingly, economists have realized that "institutions matter" because they influence economic activities. Increasingly, too, economics is used to improve our understanding of how institutions and how legal systems work. This new Palgrave Pivot series studies the intersection between law and economics, and addresses the need for greater interaction between the two disciplines.

Aurelien Portuese

The Battle for the Future of Antitrust

Brandeis, Bork, and Schumpeter

palgrave
macmillan

Aurelien Portuese
GW Competition & Innovation Lab
The George Washington University
Washington, DC, USA

Compass Lexecon
Washington, DC, USA

ISSN 2662-6535 ISSN 2662-6543 (electronic)
Palgrave Studies in Institutions, Economics and Law
ISBN 978-3-031-75793-8 ISBN 978-3-031-75794-5 (eBook)
https://doi.org/10.1007/978-3-031-75794-5

This Palgrave Macmillan imprint is published by the registered company Springer Nature Switzerland AG
The registered company address is: Gewerbestrasse 11, 6330 Cham, Switzerland

Table of Cases

- *Standard Oil Co. of New Jersey v. United States*, 221 U.S. 1 (1911).
- *United States v. United States Steel Corp.*, 251 U.S. 417 (1920).
- *United States v. International Harvester Co.*, 274 U.S. 693 (1927).
- *Chicago Board of Trade v. United States*, 246 U.S. 231 (1918).
- *United States v. Aluminum Co. of America*, 148 F.2d 416 (1945).
- *United States v. Grinnell Corp.*, 384 U.S. 563 (1966).
- Reiter v. Sonotone Corp., 442 U.S. 330, 343 (1979).
- United States v. General Dynamics Corp., 415 U.S. 486 (1974).
- United States v. Marine Bancorporation, Inc., 418 U.S. 602 (1974).
- Cargill v. Monfort, 479 U.S. 104 (1986).
- *United States v. Bertelsmann SE & Co*, 646 F. Supp. 3d 1 (2022).
- *Illumina, Inc. v. FTC*, 88 F.4th 1036, 2023.
- *In the Matter of Illumina Inc. and GRAIL*, FTC No 9401, March 2021.
- *In the Matter of Illumina Inc. and GRAIL*, FTC Initial Decision, September 9, 2022.
- *Illumina, Inc. v. FTC*, 88 F.4th 1036, (2023).
- *United States v. JetBlue Airways Corp*, _F.Supp.3d_ (2024).
- *United States v. Philadelphia Nat'l Bank*, 374 U.S. 321, 367 (1963)
- *Brown Shoe Co. v. United States*, 370 U.S. 294, 317–18 (1962).
- *FTC v. IQVIA Holdings Inc.*, No. 1:23-civ-06188-ER, ECF No. 324 (Dec. 29, 2023).

- *United States v. First Nat'l Bank & Trust Co. of Lexington*, 376 U.S. 665, 669–670 (1964) (per curiam)
- United States v. American Tobacco Co., 221 U.S. 106 (1911).
- United States v. E. I. Du Pont De Nemours & Co., 188 F. 127 (3d Cir. 1911).
- United States v. Lehigh Valley R.R., 254 U.S. 255 (1920).
- United States v. Trans-Missouri Freight Ass'n, 166 U.S. 290 (1897).
- Northern Securities Co. v. United States, 193 U.S. 197 (1904).
- United States v. Lehigh Valley R.R., 254 U.S. 255 (1920).
- United States v. Pabst Brewing Co., 384 U.S. 546 (1966).
- United States v. Von's Grocery Co., 384 U.S. 270 (1966).
- United States v. Grinnell Corp. 384 U.S. 563, 57071 (1966).
- European Commission v. CK Telecoms UK Investments Ltd., Case C-376/20 P, 13 July 2023 (European Court of Justice).
- Utah Pie. Co. Continental Baking Co., 386 U.S. 685, 87 S.Ct. 1326 (1967).
- Kodak Co. v. Image Technical Services, Inc., 504 U.S. 451 (1992)
- Verizon Communications, Inc. v. Law Offices of Curtis V. Trinko, LLP, 540 US 398 (2003).
- United Brands Company and United Brands Continentaal BV v Commission of the European Communities. - Chiquita Bananas. - Case 27/76 (1978).
- Hoffmann-La Roche v. Commission, 1979 E.C.R. 461 (1979).
- United States v. Microsoft (D.C. Cir. 2001) 253 F.3d 34, 49.
- U.S. v. Bayer AG, et al (D.D.C. 2019).
- Oscar Brönner v. Mediaprint, Case C-7/97, [1999], CMLR 4 112.
- Radio Telefis Eireann v. Commission, Case 76-77R, 91/98R [1989] ECR 1141, [1989] 4 CMLR 749.
- United States v. Aluminum Co. of America, 148 F.2d 416 (1945).
- Case C-170/13, Huawei Technologies Co. Ltd v. ZTE Corp. and ZTE Deutschland GmbH [2015], EU:C:2015:477.
- Slovak Telekom a.s., v. European Commission, Case C-165/19 P (2021).
- Case AT.39985 – Motorola, European Commission's decision of April 29, 2014.
- Brooke Grp. Ltd. v. Brown & Williamson Tobacco Corp., 509 U.S. 209, 224 (1993).
- EU Court of First Instance Decision on Case T-342/99, Airtours v Commission, ECR II-2585 (2002).

In an era teetering on the brink of seismic change, the future of antitrust laws hangs precariously in the balance. Once steadfastly anchored by decades of dominant economic analysis, these laws are now being violently uprooted by a revolutionary Brandeisian storm. This paradigmatic upheaval has plunged antitrust into a vortex of instability. For, this dramatic shift has cast us into a void of instability, where the foundations that were once strong are deteriorating. Radical changes erode antitrust's ability to offer the steadfast guidelines crucial for fostering predictability and safeguarding the lifeblood of progress: innovation. Not only is the stability of antitrust's historic journey at stake, but also the very essence of fostering innovation within the cauldron of a cutthroat economy. The battle lines for the heart and soul of antitrust are deeply etched; at stake is not merely the stability of its historic journey but the very essence of fostering innovation within the cauldron of a competitive economy.

In the past, the Chicago School, which is a prestigious institution, was responsible for directing the field of antitrust analysis. Its unwavering faith in the importance of economic efficiency served as the institution's guiding North Star. During the course of his groundbreaking work, "The Antitrust Paradox," the illustrious Robert Bork revealed a profound irony: antitrust, in its attempt to encourage competition, paradoxically ended up suffocating it. For a considerable amount of time, the "Borkian" approach, which is deeply rooted in economic analysis, has been able to withstand the onslaught of criticism. In recent times, however, the winds of change have brought back an old adversary: the populist antitrust approach. This adversary has been around for centuries. In remembrance of Justice Louis D. Brandeis, a visionary who eulogized the virtues of small businesses and vehemently denounced the "Curse of Bigness," this resurgent populist wave heralds a groundbreaking shift in the antitrust ideology. They have been given the name "Neo-Brandeisians." This is a shift that goes against the conventional antitrust law and economics in favor of granting broad discretionary power to reshape markets into diverse landscapes that are populated by small business units that are thriving.

On the other hand, I argue that the limitations that are inherent in the Borkian antitrust doctrine do not require a headlong dive into the arms of the populist and Brandeisian currents. The field of antitrust law is currently confronted with a significant junction: the decision that is about to be made is not a straightforward choice between the two extremes of the Brandeisian and Borkian doctrines. The relevance and vitality of economic analysis in the field of antitrust law are critically dependent on a profound and unwavering commitment to the concept of efficiency. Efficiency is an umbrella that encompasses not only the aspects of allocative and productive efficiency, but also, most importantly, the pulsating heart of innovation, which is dynamic efficiency. Keeping this principle of innovation-centricity in mind is essential for conducting an economic analysis of antitrust laws that is sensitive to both the requirements of the present and the aspirations of the future. A forward-thinking approach like this one, which is deeply rooted in the groundbreaking Schumpeterian principles, not only promises to steer clear of the perilous shoals of populist antitrust, but it also promises to realign the compass of antitrust scrutiny with the imperatives of a competitive landscape that is driven by innovation.

In this Schumpeterian world that has been envisioned, innovation goes beyond its role as a simple component and ascends to the position of the cornerstone of a revitalized economic analysis of antitrust laws. Innovation is the source of social and technological progress—it should be the source of antitrust interventions.

Innovation is best preserved by preserving and encouraging dynamic efficiencies. Fully embedding dynamic efficiencies into antitrust enforcement would contribute to an antitrust policy that avoids stifling innovation. The goal of this dynamic antitrust approach is to create a harmonious symphony between dynamic efficiencies and the fundamental principles of antitrust. This will ensure that the spirit of innovation will continue to be the powerful force that propels competition forward. This approach does not merely aim to maintain the incentives for innovation; rather, it seeks to stabilize the oscillating antitrust pendulum, providing the much-needed predictability and stability that is essential for both consumers and business owners alike. In an era in which the only thing that is consistent is change, this revitalized vision of antitrust analysis, which is firmly rooted in dynamic efficiency, serves as a beacon of hope and a guiding light. It provides a path forward that is well-balanced, one that honors the legacy of antitrust laws while enthusiastically embracing the future. This ensures that the engines of innovation will continue to propel our competitive economy toward new horizons of progress and prosperity.

Introduction

Stabilizing the Pendulum

The antitrust pendulum is swinging again. Antitrust laws—which aim at regulating competition in a market—as historically swung between two main perspectives. On the one hand, some perceive antitrust laws as a political instrument aimed at deconcentrating markets as an end in itself—the protection of small businesses thus requires a continuous restrain on the size of companies to promote competition.[1] This represents the populist view of antitrust where smallness prevails over bigness, irrespective of the economic merits of large companies, and regardless of the economic effects that a certain level of market concentration would generate to social welfare. On the other hand, some perceive antitrust law as an economic instrument to foster efficiency and maximize social welfare in the market–the protection of competition suggests that only anticompetitive conduct leading to inefficiencies justifies antitrust interventions.[2] According to this view of antitrust, economic efficiency prevails over moral and political concerns. These two perspectives correspond to two antitrust paradigms.[3]

[1] See Wu (2018); Khan (2018); Teachout (2020).

[2] Bork (1978); Posner (2001); Hovenkamp (2005).

[3] Portuese (2022); Portuese (2020).

Whereas the former paradigm largely dominated antitrust enforcement from its inception in 1890 until the 70s, the antitrust paradigm that prevailed since then was the latter: Antitrust law & economics with economic efficiency principles enjoyed academic standing and policy preferences.[4] Although there is no rigid line in history segregating the two types of paradigm, considering the existence of some exceptional rulings in certain periods, the predominant case law in the United States until the 70s pervaded other, political ideals that are not related to economic efficiency, nor the consumer welfare standard.[5]

Before the 70s and the Chicago school, some judicial decisions cannot be framed as in line with the abovementioned "populist" view. But they were exceptions, not the rule. Cases like Standard Oil[6], US Steel[7], International Harvester[8], Chicago Board of Trade[9], Alcoa[10], and United States v. Grinnell[11] illustrate these exceptions.

It was only with the rise of the commonly named (second) "Chicago School" that the majority opinion reverted to considering antitrust primary goal the pursuit to economic efficiency in a view to maximize benefits to consumers.[12] This view is noticeable in Reiter v. Sonotone[13], where the Supreme Court quoted Bork to suggest that "Congress designed the Sherman Act as a 'consumer welfare prescription'" and guided many future cases, including General Dynamics[14], Marine Bancorporation[15], and Cargill v. Monfort[16], that clearly rejected Brown Shoe's paradigm.

[4] Baker (2019).

[5] Hoffmann et al. (2020).

[6] *Standard Oil Co. of New Jersey v. United States*, 221 U.S. 1 (1911).

[7] *United States v. United States Steel Corp.*, 251 U.S. 417 (1920).

[8] *United States v. International Harvester Co.*, 274 U.S. 693 (1927).

[9] *Chicago Board of Trade v. United States*, 246 U.S. 231 (1918).

[10] *United States v. Aluminum Co. of America*, 148 F.2d 416 (1945).

[11] *United States v. Grinnell Corp.*, 384 U.S. 563 (1966).

[12] Hovenkamp (2005:39-40).

[13] Reiter v. Sonotone Corp., 442 U.S. 330, 343 (1979).

[14] United States v. General Dynamics Corp., 415 U.S. 486 (1974).

[15] United States v. Marine Bancorporation, Inc., 418 U.S. 602 (1974).

[16] Cargill v. Monfort, 479 U.S. 104 (1986).

Now, the antitrust paradigm is shifting back to the previous paradigm.[17] With it, the pendulum is swinging again, undoing years of judicial precedents, vilipending decades of regulatory enforcement, and disparaging half a century of academic literature.[18] As the pendulum swings back, antirust is shaking.[19] Its foundations are weaker than ever, its rationale is profoundly questioned, and its raison d'être is put under speculations.

The so-called new Brandeisian revolution has gained considerable momentum with the Biden Administration. What used to be a group of advocates at the fringe of academic scholarship has successfully entered the strategic roles of the Biden Administration to deliver a radical paradigm shift in the antitrust policy. President appointed Lina Khan as Chair of the Federal Trade Commission, Jonathan Kanter as head of the Department of Justice's Antitrust Division, and Tim Wu as the Special Assistant to the President for technology and competition policy. The latter was instrumental in the adoption of the Executive Order on Promoting Competition in the American Economy which instructed departments to pursue an assertive competition policy.[20] When signing the Executive Order, President Biden remarked:

> [O]ver time, we've lost the fundamental American idea that true capitalism depends on fair and open competition. Forty years ago, we chose the wrong path, in my view, following the misguided philosophy of people like Robert Bork, and pulled back on enforcing laws to promote competition. We're now 40 years into the experiment of letting giant corporations accumulate more and more power. And where—what have we gotten from it? Less growth, weakened investment, fewer small businesses. Too many Americans who feel left behind. Too many people who are poorer than their parents. I believe the experiment failed. We have to get back to an economy that grows from the bottom up and the middle out.[21]

[17] Portuese (2022).

[18] Hovenkamp (2019).

[19] Crane (2019).

[20] White House, "Executive Order on Promoting Competition in the American Economy", July 9, 2021.

[21] White House, "Remarks by President Biden at Signing of an Executive Order Promoting Competition in the American Economy", July 9, 2021.

The objective of the Brandeisian revolution is to terminate the Borkian paradigm. It is crucial to acknowledge that the Brandeisian revolution, despite its lack of stability and controversial nature, has attained certain levels of accomplishment. Furthermore, apart from political nominations and the efforts of regulatory agencies, particularly noteworthy are some wins achieved in the legal arena.

The most illustrative examples are the mergers successfully blocked in courts. The planned merger between the book publisher Penguin Random House with its competitor Simon & Schuster (1) is perhaps the most notable success, certainly because of the creative reasoning of the judge to block the merger. Other notable decisions that illustrate the temporary victory of the Brandeisian revolution include

1. *The Prohibition of the Penguin Random House-Simon & Schuster Merger.*[22] Penguin Books were created in the 30s in the United Kingdom. Founded by Sir Allen Lane, Penguin revolutionized the industry by introducing high-quality, affordable paperback books, making literature accessible to the masses. Meanwhile, across the Atlantic, Random House was being nurtured by Bennett Cerf and Donald Klopfer in the United States, focusing on the ethos of giving the author's voice a platform. Over the decades, both Penguin and Random House flourished independently, driven by innovative publishing strategies. Penguin's colorful paperbacks filled the shelves of every bookstore, while Random House grew by acquiring esteemed imprints and nurturing literary talents.

A metamorphosis occurred in 2013, with the merger of these two publishing titans, forming Penguin Random House. This merger was not just a business decision but a strategic alignment to fortify their presence in a rapidly evolving digital world. The combined entity boasted an unparalleled catalog of titles, including classics, bestsellers, and academic texts. What sets Penguin Random House apart is not just its size but its approach to publishing. It's a blend of artistic intuition and business acumen. Nurturing authors, curating diverse voices, and embracing technological advancements such as e-books and audiobooks have been pivotal in its strategy. Moreover, its commitment to sustainability, literacy,

[22] *United States v. Bertelsmann SE & Co*, 646 F. Supp. 3d 1 (2022).

and social responsibility reflects a business model that looks beyond profits. Penguin Random House stands as the largest publisher globally, boasting a significant share in the English-speaking markets. Its dominance is seen not just in sales but in its influence in literary awards, bestseller lists, and global reach. However, this giant faces its own set of challenges. The rise of independent publishers, self-publishing platforms, and changes in consumer reading habits pose constant challenges. The digital revolution, especially, requires Penguin Random House to continuously innovate and adapt.

Bertelsmann (53% of Penguin) and Pearson (47% of Random House) formed a joint venture in 2013. Each firm has "exclusive" rights and constraints to protect each party in Penguin Random House (PRH). Online distribution changes books. As books, music, and newspapers lose revenue, established publishers seek a new paradigm. The Internet revolutionized book sales. Amazon began online business with global book shipping. Even though publishers had trouble setting foreign prices, buyers bought books. E-book delivery, the second internet paradigm, hurts book sales. Publishers may have sold more e-books. Prices have dropped because e-books have low marginal production and delivery costs. Accessibility enhanced book sales. Publishers sell e-books via Amazon, Apple, and Barnes & Noble. Despite their passive role in innovation, new internet models demand publishers to access writers and back catalogues. Trend likely to end. Some will want to kill publishers' sales.

When Paramount's ViacomCBS, the parent company, decided to sell Simon & Schuster in 2020, it was widely expected that one of the other big publishers would purchase the company, resulting in the consolidation of the Big Five publishers into the Big Four. PRH and HarperCollins emerged as the last contenders in the auction, and PRH emerged victorious with a reported bid of $2.2 billion. This consolidation trend worried the DOJ's Antitrust Division, not only for the reduction of a competitor in an oligopolistic market, but also and most creatively, for the monopsony effects of the merger. The merger between two of the Big Five US book publishers—Hachette, HarperCollins, Macmillan, Penguin Random House, and Simon & Schuster—was already predicted to lead to antitrust concern. But, the idea that the merger would create a buyer's monopoly (i.e., monopsony) enabling the merged entity to suppress authors' wages and treat them unfairly was novel. Antitrust agencies have rarely sued based on monopsony effects—but the Biden Administration was keen to go down light-traveled roads and argue the case before Biden-appointed judge, Judge Florence Pan from the US District Court for the District of Columbia.

She unequivocally sided with Jonathan Kanter's DOJ Antitrust Division and considered that the merger would lessen competition in the market to acquire publishing rights and therefore violated Section 7 of the Clayton Act. The Department of Justice contended that the merger would be detrimental to competition in the acquisition of publication rights to "anticipated top-selling books," which would result in smaller advances for the authors of such books and contract terms that were less conducive to their interests. The defendants, PRH and S&S, did not contest the fact that if advances are drastically reduced, some authors will be unable to write. This will lead to a reduction in the number of books that are published, a reduction in the range of ideas that are available in the market, and an unavoidable loss of intellectual and creative production. Nevertheless, they argued that the merger would not have a negative impact on competition and that advances would instead increase after the merger. They disputed the notion that progress would fall after the merger. The judge agreed with the Department of Justice's definition of the relevant market, which was the publishing rights to expected best-selling novels. Judge Pan explained that:

> [t]he government's case sounds in 'monopsony,' a market condition where a buyer with too much market power can lower prices or otherwise harm sellers. Essentially, the government alleges that the merger will increase market concentration in the publishing industry, which will allow publishing companies to pay certain authors less money for the rights to publish their books.

Taking into consideration the potential for harm to intellectual and creative production, the decision is noteworthy from the point of view of innovation since it acknowledges the possibility that authors may earn lower advances and, as a result, be less able to create. In the publishing sector, this might lead to a decrease in the number of books that are published and a reduction in the range of ideas that are available for purchase, both of which would be bad for innovation. To reach the conclusion of the detrimental monopsonist effects of the merger, Judge Pan agreed with the DOJ's narrow market definition and thus risks wage suppression on top-selling authors and stated:

> Contrary to the defendants' contentions, the relevant market appropriately identifies a submarket of targeted sellers—the authors of anticipated top-selling books. Those authors have unique needs and preferences, have fewer outlets that can satisfy their requirements, and therefore are vulnerable to anticompetitive behavior.

Due to the fact that it entails the use of monopsony theory in a case where the Department of Justice has typically concentrated on monopoly theory, the decision is considered unconventional. In addition to this, it acknowledges the possibility of causing harm to competition on the buy-side of the market, which is a component of antitrust law that is less frequently addressed.

> The government's focus on advances to the world's best-paid authors instead of consumers or the intense competitiveness in the publishing sector runs contrary to its mission to ensure fair competition, "Random House said, expressing disagreement with the findings. Unsurprisingly, this might set a highly important precedent due to its emphasis on the effects of monopsonistic behavior on labor. Since the Biden administration's antitrust enforcement primarily targets monopolies, this judgment may have far-reaching consequences on sectors as diverse as healthcare, college athletics, big tech, and Hollywood, as we've already covered on Competition Corner. "The antitrust laws protect competition for the acquisition of goods and services for workers." Assistant Attorney General Jonathan Kanter proclaimed Judge Pan's decision a "victory for authors, the marketplace of ideas, consumers, and competitive markets." It is undoubtedly a victory for the Brandeisian revolution. In defending the merger, defendants argued that a private equity company that does not understand the publishing business could acquire S&S. Rebuffing these arguments as "not relevant", Judge Pan considered that merger analysis provide no room to "contemplate consideration of the preferences of the merging parties' employees and stakeholders, or their distaste for other potential buyers of the assets in question." Judge Pan added that "the Court notes that the expressed concerns about a private-equity acquisition are highly speculative.

Judge Pan's opinion was delivered on October 31, 2022. Exactly one year after the judge considered a private-equity acquisition of S&S to be "highly speculative," on October 30, 2023, it was announced that the private-equity firm KKR acquired S&S.[23] KKR acquired S&S from Paramount for $1.62 billion, down from the $2.2 billion offered by PRH.

2. *The Prohibition of the Illumina-Grail Merger.*[24] Illumina, Inc. is a leading firm in the field of genomics. David Walt, Larry Bock, John Stuelpnagel, Anthony Czarnik, and Mark Chee were the individuals that initially introduced the corporation to the world on April 1, 1998. Through its history, Illumina has achieved a number of key milestones and introduced a number of advancements. Shankar Balasubramanian and David Klenerman, two scientists from Cambridge, were able to see the movements of a polymerase at the single molecule level by employing fluorescently labeled nucleotides back in the middle of the 1990s. Illumina's sequencing by synthesis (SBS) technology is a product of this study, which led to its development. One gigabase (Gb) of data could be sequenced in a single run with the first Solexa sequencer, which was called the Genome Analyzer and was released in the year 2006. In the beginning of 2007, Illumina made the acquisition of Solexa, and ever since then, the technology has been utilized to sequence a great number of genomes associated with microbes, plants, humans, and animals.

Almost 80% of the gene-sequencing market is controlled by Illumina, which gives the company a strong position in the market for next-generation sequencing (NGS). The valuation of the company is greater than $16.6 billion, and despite difficult years, Illumina continued to invest in genomic research centers, pharmaceutical businesses, academic institutions, and clinical research organizations.

Interestingly, Illumina founded GRAIL in 2016 as a standalone business that it owns a majority of. The objective was to measure blood circulating nucleic acids directly in order to establish a pan-cancer screening test. With participation from Bezos Expeditions, Bill Gates, and Sutter Hill Ventures, GRAIL was originally financed with over $100 million in Series A financing from Illumina and ARCH Venture. Later, the business

[23] Elizabeth A. Harris, Alexandra Alter, "KKR Closes Deal to Buy Simon & Schuster", *The New York Times*, October 30, 2023.

[24] *Illumina, Inc. v. FTC*, 88 F.4th 1036, 2023.

was split off in order to collect money for the multi-cancer early detection test (MCED) to be tested in clinical settings.

Illumina declared its plan to purchase GRAIL in September 2020. The purchase was made with the intention of quickening the commercialization of the Galleri cancer blood test, which was scheduled to debut in 2021. Galleri was able to identify the source tissue with 99% specificity and detect over 50 malignancies in all stages, according to Illumina. In 2021, Illumina terminated their acquisition of Grail before the European regulators finished their antitrust investigation. Illumina presented strong arguments for rejoining GRAIL. The purchase, according to the business, would allow it to expand its offering to encompass cancer diagnosis, cancer monitoring, and cancer screening, resulting in a portfolio of best-in-class solutions for the whole cancer care continuum. Illumina also thought that the combination would spur innovation and be beneficial to competition.

Nevertheless, there were a lot of regulatory obstacles to the transaction. In March 2021, the Federal Trade Commission (FTC) protested Illumina's acquisition of Grail, claiming that the transaction will increase costs and stifle innovation in the multi-cancer early detection (MCED) test market in the United States. Additionally, the European Commission banned the agreement, claiming that Illumina would be motivated to deny Grail's competitors access to its technology or otherwise harm them, although the European Union (EU)'s ability to block the merger was controversial due to the absence of business activity of GRAIL in the EU.[25] Despite these obstacles, Illumina completed the transaction before receiving regulatory permission, which resulted in a sizable fine.

In the United States, the FTC challenged the acquisition of the GRAIL by Illumina before its Administrative Law Judge (ALJ)—the FTC's internal judge. The FTC challenged the merger due to Illumina's alleged incentives to exclude GRAIL's rivals from the NGS platform, especially Galleri. The FTC alleged that:

> "Grail's rivals have no alternative to using Illumina's NGS platforms to develop and commercialize their MCED tests, therefore, they will be unable to divert away from Illumina if the combined firm raises their costs or otherwise forecloses or disadvantages them. As a result, after the Acquisition, Illumina will control the fate of every potential rival to Grail for

[25] Portuese (2023).

> the foreseeable future. Post-Acquisition, Illumina will have the ability to monitor each company developing an MCED test using its NGS platform and the incentive to kill or disable any products that appear likely to take significant business away from Galleri."[26]

The FTC alleged novel theories of harm, especially harm to innovation and the acquisition of GRAIL as a potential competitor to Illumina:

> "Allowing Illumina to purchase Grail and act on the incentives created by the Acquisition would cause substantial harm to U.S. consumers, who would experience reduced innovation, as well as potentially higher costs and reduced choice and quality for these life-saving products."

Nevertheless, the FTC's own judge—the ALJ—rejected the FTC's arguments and considered that the FTC "has failed to prove its asserted prima facie case that Illumina's post-Acquisition ability and incentive to advantage Grail to the disadvantage of Grail's alleged rivals is likely to result in a substantial lessening of competition in the relevant market for the research, development, and commercialization of MCED test."[27] Additionally, the ALJ considered that in a harsh tone that:

> "Absent proof of a likelihood of harm to Grail's alleged competitors in the reasonably near future, Complaint Counsel's argument that such harm will further result in likely harm to existing innovation and future commercial competition is deprive of its factual premise. As state in Arch Coal, 329 F. Supp. 2d at 116, "antitrust theory and speculation cannot trump fact [...]"[28]

[26] *In the Matter of Illumina Inc. and GRAIL*, FTC No 9401, March 2021.

[27] *In the Matter of Illunima Inc. and GRAIL*, FTC Initial Decision, September 9, 2022.

[28] Id.

But, the FTC fought for the divestiture and won[29]: in what it considered to be "major win for the FTC"[30], the FTC managed to force Illumina to divest GRAIL.

Despite the scrutiny of the EU and the FTC, Illumina finalized its $8 billion acquisition of Grail in August 2021. In accordance with the divestment order issued by the European Commission, the divestiture will be carried out through a capital markets transaction or third-party sale to settle the conditions by the end of the second quarter of 2024. Illumina has decided not to challenge the Fifth Circuit's ruling any further after reading the Court's ruling.

The European Union fined Illumina a record €432 million in July for terminating its acquisition of Grail before receiving EU antitrust permission. Francis de Souza, the former CEO of Illumina, resigned as a result of the firm being embroiled in a proxy spat with activist investor Carl Icahn on its $7.1 billion acquisition of Grail, a manufacturer of cancer tests that has encountered regulatory obstacles.

Beyond these multiple events, the judicial decision reversing the ALJ's decision illustrates a change in antitrust analysis since the Biden Administration. Indeed, the judge considered that Illumina would have the ability and incentive to harm the innovation capabilities of GRAIL's rivals:

> "What makes the Illumina-Grail merger especially problematic is that rival MCED test developers depend on access to Illumina's NGS platforms and have no available substitutes, now or in the near future. That gives the merged entity the ability to tilt the playing field in Grail's favor in multiple ways, and the merged firm has a strong incentive to do whatever it can to keep other MCED test developers at least one step behind Grail in the innovation race."[31]

Considering that the claimed efficiencies were not merger-specific, the judge rejected Illumina's claims that efficiencies will be "passed along to consumers." This decision is a considerable victory for the FTC's new

[29] In April 2023, the FTC overturned the Administrative Law Judge's decision to dismiss the case and mandated that Illumina to sell Grail. Illumina filed a petition with the Fifth Circuit in June 2023, requesting a review of the Commission's order and opinion.

[30] Federal Trade Commission, "Statement Regarding Illumina's Decision to Divest Grail", December 18, 2023.

[31] *Illumina, Inc. v. FTC*, 88 F.4th 1036, (2023).

approach to mergers in general, and vertical mergers in particular, where harms to innovation (defined as the risks for potential rivals to be deprived of fair chances to innovate) becomes a new theory of harm justifying prohibiting what previous Administrations would have considered as a pro-competitive merger. This shift is notable since it is endorsed by the judiciary. This judicial trend is confirmed with the prohibition of the Jet Blue Airways and Spirit Airlines merger.

3. *The Prohibition of the Jet Blue Airways-Spirit Airlines Merger.*[32] JetBlue and Spirit, the sixth and seventh largest airlines in the United States, were respectively barred from merging by Judge William Young, a Reagan-appointed judge. Notable is the fact that the prohibition was issued by a long-serving Republican judge, thereby validating the new approach of Brandeisian leadership to vertical mergers of the Biden Administration, and that it is one of the rarest blocked mergers in the airline industry. After the blocked merger, Spirit Airlines may go bankrupt—spelling a possibly embarrassing outcome for antitrust agencies. But how did the agencies manage to block the merger in the first place?

To better understand the prohibition ruling from Judge Young, it is important to come back to the beginning of Jet Blue Airways. August 1998 saw David Neeleman begin JetBlue Airways as "NewAir." The Delaware-incorporated company is based in Forest Hills, Queens[1]. JetBlue commenced flights from JFK on February 11, 2000. The airline, like Southwest, provided low tickets but added amenities including in-flight entertainment, TV at every seat, and Sirius XM satellite radio. Airlines service over 100 North American, Latin American, Caribbean, and European destinations

JetBlue's main competitors are Southwest, Delta, United, and American. These four airlines control 80% of the US domestic market. JetBlue CEO Robin Hayes expects 5% market share. JetBlue struggles despite growth. For example, the airline lost $153 million in Q3 2023 due to operational difficulties and a US seat oversupply.

In opposite, Spirit Airlines is more of a legacy airline: Spirit Airlines was created in 1964 under the name Clippert Trucking Company, which was

[32] *United States v. JetBlue Airways Corp*, _F.Supp.3d_ (2024).

originally based in Michigan. The company commenced its air charter operations in 1980 under the name Charter One. Spirit Airlines was established in 1992 when Charter One incorporated jet aircraft into its operations. Spirit Airlines initiated service to Orlando, Fort Lauderdale, and St. Petersburg, Florida, subsequently expanding its operations to include additional cities.

Spirit Airlines is a prominent American airline in the ultra-low-cost air travel market in the United States. Regularly scheduled flights are offered in the United States, Caribbean, and Latin America. In 2023, Spirit ranked as the seventh largest passenger carrier in North America, its primary competitors of the airline being American, Delta, Allegiant, WestJet, United, and Alaska Airlines. Spirit Airlines has faced difficulties despite its success: the airline has reduced prices, particularly during off-peak periods, as a result of increased personnel salaries, other expenses, and the growing capacity of domestic aircraft.

Spirit was experiencing financial difficulties and had not yet fully recovered from the economic impact of the 2020 pandemic when it entered into a contractual agreement with JetBlue in July 2022. Spirit pursued a merger with JetBlue in order to enhance its financial situation. This envisaged merger would continue the consolidation trends that took place in the US market.

Indeed, the US airline market has seen significant transformation in the previous three decades due to strategic mergers and acquisitions. These strategic maneuvers have significantly transformed the aviation industry, particularly in the aftermath of the September 11 attacks. An important aspect of airline consolidation occurred when American Airlines acquired Trans World Airlines in January 2001. The acquisition of TWA, a company that had multiple bankruptcies and had a significant presence at JFK Airport, marked the conclusion of its operations. The acquisition was finalized in December 2001, resulting in the decline of TWA. This merger exemplifies the initial concentration of the business, as larger airlines assimilated smaller ones.

In 2005, America West Airlines, headquartered in Arizona, acquired US Airways, marking another significant consolidation in the airline industry. In contrast to the American-TWA merger, US Airways maintained its brand, while America West's brand was terminated. This merger exemplifies the dominance of one airline's brand, particularly in terms of market familiarity. In 2008, Delta Airlines and Northwest Airlines combined, furthering the process of consolidation. As a result of this merger, Delta briefly became the largest airline globally, highlighting the increasing significance of airline consolidation. In 2010, the Northwest trademark was eliminated, indicating the fall of prominent airlines.

The merger between United Airlines and Continental Airlines commenced in 2008, including intricate processes. The airlines joined in 2010 after engaging in negotiations and considering other merger options. United retained its name, but its livery underwent a modification to incorporate Continental's globe, reflecting the amalgamation of the two airlines. In 2010, Southwest Airlines acquired AirTran Airways. Southwest acquired this company in 2011 in order to increase its market share. Southwest saw significant growth by 2014 with the decommissioning of AirTran, indicating that mergers were not exclusive to conventional airlines. American Airlines made another significant merger attempt with US Airways almost ten years after merging with TWA, with the goal of surpassing Delta as the largest airline globally. The merger, initiated in early 2013 and finalized in December 2013, exemplifies the consolidation of the airline industry to create larger and more competitive global carriers.

The merger between Frontier Airlines and Spirit Airlines in 2022 heralded a new era in the consolidation of airlines. The formation of this merger, resulting in the establishment of the fifth-largest airline in the United States, exemplifies the ongoing consolidation within the airline industry. The merger between Spirit Airlines and Frontier Airlines, with an estimated value of over $2.8 billion, was terminated in July 2022. Subsequently, JetBlue presented an offer to acquire Spirit Airlines without being asked, proposing a higher valuation. JetBlue's proposal contained a cash offer of $33.50 per share, resulting in a cumulative sum of $3.8 billion. Spirit Airlines has agreed to accept this offer, and the merger is anticipated to be finalized by January 2024. Nevertheless, the consolidation was impeded by a federal judge in January 2024.

In the last three decades, the consolidation of airlines through mergers and acquisitions has resulted in the concentration of market dominance among a small number of big carriers. The change in competition has had an impact on the operations of airlines, their dominance in the market, and the choices available to customers. These mergers have facilitated airlines in achieving economies of scale and attaining global recognition, but they also give rise to apprehensions regarding market competition and the interests of air travel consumers. But, these concentration trends in the airline industry are the very basis for Judge Young to have blocked the Jet Blue-Spirit merger.

Recognizing that it is "almost impossible to predict" the future of the airline industry, Judge Young made "its best attempt" to do so when prohibiting the merger.[33] Judge Young starts with the observation of the market structure:

> "The airline industry is an oligopoly that has become more concentrated due to a series of mergers in the first decades of the twenty-first century, with a small group of firms in control of the vast majority of the market."[34] This oligopolistic market structure of the airline industry leads to the concern that "if JetBlue were permitted to gobble up Spirit—at least as proposed—it would eliminate one of the airline industry's few primary competitors that provides unique innovation and price discipline." The merger may enable the merged entity to compete with large carriers (such as United, or American Airlines) but would also "incentivize JetBlue further to abandon its roots as a maverick, low-cost carrier", thereby harming consumers. It is these concentration trends in the airline industry, partly due to the series of mergers mentioned, that led to an oligopolistic market structure having the "tendency to monopoly"[35]

The concentration trends and the series of merger in the airline industry led Judge Young to revert to old cases from the 60s such as Philadelphia National Bank and Brown Shoe in order to "arrest the trend toward concentration."[36] The reading of the Clayton Act is a fundamental victory for the Brandeisians, eager to revigorate what they consider to be "controlling precedents" which enabled the prohibition of mergers even when the merging firms have small market shares and try to compete against incumbents.

[33] *United States v. JetBlue Airways Corp*, _F.Supp.3d_ (2024).

[34] Id.

[35] Id, citing *United States v. Philadelphia Nat'l Bank*, 374 U.S. 321, 367 (1963).

[36] *United States v. Philadelphia Nat'l Bank*, 374 U.S. 321, 367 (1963); *Brown Shoe Co. v. United States*, 370 U.S. 294, 317–18 (1962).

4. *The Prohibition of IQVIA's Acquisition of Propel Media*.[37] The FTC filed a lawsuit against IQVIA's acquisition of Propel Media, arguing that the merger will reduce strong competition between the two companies. This is due to the fact that Propel Media and IQVIA are two of the top three providers of programmatic advertising services in the healthcare industry. The FTC alleged in an administrative complaint that the proposed acquisition would provide IQVIA with a market-leading position in programmatic advertising that is directed toward physicians and other health care professionals. In addition, the Commission gave the FTC staff the authority to petition the federal district court for a preliminary injunction and a temporary restraining order in order to prevent IQVIA from finalizing its acquisition of Propel Media while the agency is still in the process of conducting its administrative proceeding. The request for a preliminary injunction that was submitted by the FTC to prevent IQVIA from acquiring Propel Media, Inc. was granted by the United States District Court for the Southern District of New York on December 29, 2023. This FTC's victory was lauded as a "win" against "an anticompetitive merger that would raise health care prices for consumers."[38]

IQVIA argued that the acquisition of Propel Media's DeepIntent would boost competition in healthcare advertising as it competes with online giants like Google, Amazon, and The Trade Desk, and would benefit healthcare providers, consumers, and the US economy. DeepIntent is a healthcare marketing technology startup that believes digital media may improve health outcomes. But the FTC argued that the acquisition would enable IQVIDIA to establish its dominant position in the market of programmatic advertising aimed at healthcare professionals. IQVIDIA and Propel Media do this through their respective platforms, Lasso Marketing and DeepIntent. The FTC considered that the merger would limit direct competition between these two organizations, which

[37] *FTC v. IQVIA Holdings Inc.*, No. 1:23-civ-06188-ER, ECF No. 324 (Dec. 29, 2023).

[38] FTC, Statement on FTC Win Securing Temporary Block of IQVIA's Acquisition of Propel Media, January 3, 2024.

might ultimately result in increased prices, worsen quality, and offer fewer options to healthcare professionals.

As a result of this horizontal merger, which is defined as a combination of two companies operating in the same industry, the FTC believes that the level of competition between DeepIntent and Lasso will be significantly reduced, and the market for digital healthcare advertising will become more concentrated. At the same time, the FTC has relied on a vertical theory of harm founded on the fact that IQVIA is a provider of essential data for digital healthcare advertising. After consideration of the evidence presented, the Court concluded that the horizontal theory of harm articulated by the FTC is likely to succeed and ruled in favor of preliminary injunctive relief.

Although the Court appeared not convinced by the FTC's vertical theory of harm, the Court endorsed the FTC's horizontal theory of harm in a Brandeisian manner—namely, by relying on the Brown Shoe indicia of 1962. Also, the FTC convinced the court that the FTC post-merger market share of DeepIntent and Lasso would exceed both the 30% threshold as articulated by the Philadelphia National Bank case of 1963. The FTC demonstrated that the merging companies compete head-to-head, and that this competition would be eliminated by the proposed merger.

5. *The New Merger Guidelines.*[39] Besides some wins in Court, the Neo-Brandeisians have managed to adopt in 2023 new Merger Guidelines that hack back to pre-Borkian era while integrating the modern issues of digital markets. Indeed, supplanting the 2010 Horizontal Merger Guidelines and the 2020 Vertical Merger Guidelines, the Neo-Brandeisians have achieved the considerable task of returning to a less economic approach with a consolidated set of merger guidelines which emphasize market structure rather than efficiency considerations and economic modeling.

Explaining that the new Merger Guidelines are "faithful to the law and reflect how competition plays out in our modern markets," Assistant Attorney General Jonathan Kanter argued that these guidelines aim at

[39] Department of Justice, Federal Trade Commission, Merger Guidelines, December 18, 2023. (hereafter "2023 Merger Guidelines").

fostering "competitive markets" while FTC Chair Lina Khan emphasized that "the 2023 Merger Guidelines reflect the new realities of how firms do business in the modern economy and ensure fidelity to statutory text and precedent."[40] Two features characterize the new Merger Guidelines:

i. The so-called "fidelity" to Congressional intent to the allegedly controlling precedents;
ii. The reflection of market realities in the modern economy.

These features explain why the Merger Guidelines is a return to a structuralist approach that characterized the 60s and why so many old cases prior to the economic analysis of antitrust law are cited, but also explain additional concerns included in the merger analysis to justify a more assertive approach (such as labor effects, platform competition, serial acquisitative firms, as well as a skeptical approach to efficiency defenses).

Indeed, as a coronation document of the new Brandeisian Movement, the 2023 Merger Guidelines reinstated the legal presumption from the 1963 Philadelphia National Bank case that mergers leading to the creation of a firm with a more than 30% market share are illegal.[41] Also, strong competitive constraint in the market may justify blocking the merger since it may remove "substantial competition" between the merging firms.[42] A new concept is the elimination of a maverick (or disruptive competitor) as increasing coordination risks post-merger, thereby justifying blocking the merger.[43] Similarly, the guidelines put an emphasis on preventing mergers that would undermine potential competition by eliminating a "potential entrant" in the market. The 2010 and the 2020 Merger Guidelines barely mentioned the lessening of competition through the elimination of a potential entrant. The 2023 Merger Guidelines articulate the loss of potential competition as justifying prohibiting mergers in two

[40] Department of Justice, "Justice Department and Federal Trade Commission Release 2023 Merger Guidelines", December 18, 2023, https://www.justice.gov/opa/pr/justice-department-and-federal-trade-commission-release-2023-merger-guidelines.

[41] Guideline 1, 2023 Merger Guidelines.

[42] Guideline 2, 2023 Merger Guidelines, (quoting *United States v. First Nat'l Bank & Trust Co. of Lexington*, 376 U.S. 665, 669-70 (1964) (per curiam)).

[43] Guidelines 3, 2023 Merger Guidelines.

ways: (i) the loss of actual potential competition when the merger eliminates a "reasonably probable future entry" and (ii) the loss of perceived potential competition when the merger lessens the "current competitive pressure."[44] To be clear, the new Merger Guidelines consider that "even an attenuate source of competition such as a potential entrant"—namely, a highly unlikely entrant—"may substantially lessen competition in [oligopolistic] markets." In other words, the threshold to qualify as potential entrant, hence bar the merger, lowers as the scrutinized market portrays oligopolistic features. Consequently, narrow market definition may lead to define many markets as oligopolistic which, in turn, will enable the agencies to block mergers on the basis of the merger involving a potential entrant.

Also, the Merger Guidelines classically refer to unlawful mergers when they may limit access to products or services that downstream rivals may need, but reveal the Neo-Brandeisian's emphasis on structure and "trends" toward vertical integration as factors to consider when blocking mergers involving critical assets or services.[45] This is particularly the focus on Guideline 7 where the agencies, departing from previous Merger Guidelines which focused on the scrutinized merger taken in isolation, adopt a holistic approach where "trends" toward concentration, either through internal growth or through "multiple mergers" are indicia for potentially unlawful mergers.[46]

This notion of "multiple mergers" in an industry or market is narrowed down to the level of the firm with Guideline 8 which prevents firms to engage in "a strategy of serial acquisitions"[47]. Thus, mergers that would otherwise be pro-competitive could be considered unlawful because the merging firms' history epitomize a pattern of "consolidation through acquisition."

Reflecting the "modern" realities, Guideline 9 states that mergers involving multi-sided platforms will involve assessment of competition for the market (inter-platform competition), competition on the market (intra-platform competition), and competition to displace the platform services on the platform (prohibition of anti-steering clauses). Although

[44] Id.

[45] Guideline 5, 2023 Merger Guidelines.

[46] Guideline 7, 2023 Merger Guidelines.

[47] Guideline 8, 2023 Merger Guidelines.

the Agencies overlook the fact that the protection of one type of competition often comes at the expense of the other type of competition on the platform (e.g., the reduction of intra-platform competition may help differentiation across platforms and thus foster inter-platform competition), Guideline 9 promises to be a particularly acute guideline given the Agencies' focus on high-tech and pharmaceutical industries.

In the same vein of these "modern" realities, Guideline 10 provides the most originality by emphasizing the monopsony effects of some mergers[48] while Guideline 11 emphasizes the antitrust concerns as a result of partial acquisitions and cross-ownership. It can be said that Guideline 11 goes further than the Celler-Kefauver Amendment to the Clayton Act as it scrutinizes the competition effects of acquisitions involving "less-than-full control." In that regard, it is questionable whether the antitrust agencies have the constitutional authority to do what an Act of Congress can do only—namely, to extend the antitrust scrutiny to mergers not resulting in a non-controlling acquisitions of the target assets. Here the Neo-Brandeisian's ambitions reach the limits of the Congressional intent and push the boundaries of what antitrust agencies can (and should) do. Be that as it may, Guideline 11 makes explicit that "cross-ownership and common ownership can reduce competition by softening firms' incentives to compete, even absent any specific anticompetitive act or intent." Reliance on Guideline 11 to block mergers will inevitably prove controversial not only on antitrust grounds, but also on constitutional grounds.

Perhaps the most illustrative aspect of the 2023 Merger Guidelines when it comes to the Neo-Brandeisian approach as a return to pre-Borkian antitrust is the high skepticism toward efficiency arguments and any rebuttal evidence that merging firms may put forward. Indeed, the 2023 Merger Guidelines put a double threshold for efficiency claims:

i. Efficiencies must be procompetitive as well as cognizable efficiencies. Efficiencies are procompetitive when they are merger-specific, verifiable, prevent the risk of a substantial lessening of competition in the relevant market, and are not resulting in an "anticompetitive worsening of terms for the merged firms' trading partners"; and

[48] Guideline 10, 2023 Merger Guidelines.

ii. Procompetitive efficiencies must be cognizable efficiencies. Cognizable efficiencies mean that the procompetitive efficiencies are of "nature, magnitude, and likelihood" so that the considered merger will not lessen competition in the relevant market. In other words, efficiencies must not only be procompetitive (qualitative and subjective assessment) but must also be cognizable (quantitative and objective assessment). It is obvious that the evidentiary threshold for merging firms to prove procompetitive efficiencies from the merger and their ability to put forward convincing rebuttal evidence against a presumption of illegality of the merger has dramatically increased with the 2023 Merger Guidelines compared to the 2010 and 2020 Merger Guidelines.

When it comes to the frequently tumultuous waters of corporate regulation, the development of the Neo-Brandeisian movement stands out as a momentous paradigm shift, a lighthouse of transformational thought. This innovative movement has accomplished a remarkable feat by re-engineering the very underpinnings of agency operations, and their crowning achievement is the crystallization of the visionary 2023 Merger Guidelines. These recommendations are not only a collection of regulations; rather, they are a daring reinvention of how we approach corporate mergers. They represent a genuine commitment to social justice, despite the fact that efficiency and innovation are still important concerns. The question remains, however, whether the judicial system, despite @@anecdotical wins, will structurally accept this aggressive attitude in the middle of this revolutionary transformation. This question is significant since the Neo-Brandeisians' meteoric rise may have preceded their projected fall, despite the fact that they have only won a few cases in court.

The Neo-Brandeisian movement is more than just a shift in antitrust thought; it is an intellectual revolution, a trumpet call to challenge the formerly untouchable principles of the Chicago School and, more specifically, the Borkian approach to antitrust. At its very core, the Neo-Brandeisian movement is more than just a shift in antitrust philosophy. The cause of redistributive justice is championed by this movement, which advocates for a fair and equal distribution of economic advantages through aggressive competition policy. Some people view this movement as a light of hope.

Neo-Brandeisians change the distribution of the value chain from consumers to independent business owners, from digital platforms to workers, and from behemoths of capital to the dynamic world of labor-intensive firms. All of these shifts are occurring simultaneously. The Neo-Brandeisians call for deconcentration not just as a policy but also as a crusade to reorganize the economic landscape in order to bring the concentration trends that innovation invariably generates under control.

Neo-Brandeisians have not only altered the narrative that is associated with antitrust, but they have also redefined it. Regulatory frameworks have been reshaped with a bold and relentless hand as a result of their impact on the highest echelons of policymaking, from the instructions of agencies to the rhetoric of presidents. Their rapid rise compels us to contemplate the future with a vigilant eye toward the future. In the process of resolving the important concerns of income inequality and market concentration, it is of utmost importance to recognize the indispensable role that innovation and efficiency play. In the face of global competition and challenges, these forces are essential because they are the lifeblood of technological progress, the cornerstones of consumer welfare, and the engines of a much-needed long-term economic growth in a time of rising competition with other global powers such as China.

We are on the verge of the day after the Neo-Brandeisians. Thus it is becoming abundantly evident that a simple return to Borkian ideas is not only unfeasible, but also intellectually and morally insufficient. The day after Neo-Brandeisians is unavoidable. Yet, it cannot be a return to Borkian antitrust. It can and should be a move toward Schumpeterian competition.

The principles of Schumpeterian competition, which I refer to as "dynamic antitrust," have the potential to shed light on this matter and should consider doing so. This approach encourages us to include the threads of dynamic innovation into the very fabric of antitrust policy, so allowing us to create a tapestry that strikes a harmonious balance between competition, efficiency, and distribution of growth opportunities. A future in which antitrust policy is not only a rulebook but rather a charter for a more just and prosperous society is the vision that is being presented here. This vision is not simply a shift in policy; rather, it is a call to embrace a future that is more inclusive, fair, and sustainable.

This book emerges not only as a scholarly work, but also as a clarion call for wisdom and foresight in the face of turbulent change. It is a book that emerges at this pivotal moment in history, when we are standing on the brink of monumental shifts in the realm of antitrust doctrines. The terrain of antitrust policy is being pounded by the ferocious winds of radical reform and the alluring allure of pendulum swings that promise a new order. Both of these forces are destroying the landscape. The lessons of history, on the other hand, reverberate loudly, warning us that these turbulent shifts frequently lead us astray, into realms of uncertainty, inefficiency, and decision-making that is short-sighted. Currently, it is a time for bravery, a time to firmly anchor the antitrust pendulum in the waters of stability, blending the everlasting wisdom of established principles with the innovative vision that is required for the future.

Against the growing tide of populist calls for a significant overhaul of antitrust laws and enforcement, it serves as a bulwark that protects against the opposition. An approach that is sophisticated, nuanced, and avoids the extremes of radical transformation is advocated for in the author's argument, which is a tapestry woven with threads of passion and pragmatism. A policy that reveres and incorporates the fundamental principle of economic efficiency while also recognizing and addressing its limitations and the necessity for its enhancement is called for by this approach. This approach does not dismiss the need for change, but rather calls for a refined and dynamic evolution of antitrust policy.

The powerful idea that economic efficiency must go beyond its traditional boundaries in order to fully embrace the concept of dynamic efficiency, which is the very heartbeat of innovation and progress, is at the center of this argument. Within the context of this vision, antitrust agencies are not merely responsible for enforcing the law; rather, they are champions of a new paradigm, one that is in accordance with the principles of dynamic antitrust. By striking a delicate balance between the steady rhythm of static efficiency and the vibrant, ever-changing melody of innovation, this revolutionary approach achieves a delicate balance. This is not merely a recommendation for policy; rather, it is a visionary blueprint for a Schumpeterian competition system, which is a celebration of the creative destruction that propels our economies forward.

During our journey through the intricate and frequently turbulent waters of economic theory and policy, this book serves as a guiding light that provides both hope and direction. It is possible for the antitrust pendulum, which has been swayed for a long time by the winds of change and controversy, to find the equilibrium that is rightfully its. In order to reach this equilibrium, it is not necessary to sacrifice the invaluable insights that come from economic expertise or the fundamental principles that underpin efficiency. In its place, it is accomplished through the process of their development, improvement, and adaptation to the ever-evolving requirements of our ever-changing world. This book does not merely propose a way forward; rather, it sheds light on a way forward for a dynamic antitrust approach that silences the voices of populist critics by utilizing the unyielding power of progress, innovation, and pragmatic foresight.

An antitrust policy that is reliable, efficient, and resistant to change in the future can be found in this document. It acts as a beacon in the midst of a storm, illuminating the path for policymakers, academics, and practitioners as they navigate the treacherous waters of economic transformation. This piece of work is not only a contribution to the field of antitrust policy; it is also a demonstration of the resiliency and adaptability of economic thought. It is a manifesto for an era in which the principles of efficiency and innovation go hand in hand, guiding us toward a future in which economic growth is balanced, equitable, and sustainable. While we are turning the pages of this book, we are not simply reading another academic treatise; rather, we are witnessing the birth of a new era in antitrust policy, one that acknowledges the past, comprehends the present, and boldly moves forward into the future.

Contents

CHAPTER 1

Borkian Antitrust Under Assault

Abstract There are several ways to approach antitrust legislation and enforcement. For example, the Chicago School of Antitrust, led by Judge Robert H. Bork, advocates for increased expertise in enforcement over economic ideologies. However, it faces constant criticism for inconsistent premises and antitrust populism. Critics argue that Borkian antitrust incorporated modern economic theories into The Sherman Act, which was likely passed at the behest of small businesses. Critics also argue that Borkian antitrust relied on unrealistic assumptions, such as perfect competition and market rivalry. Neo-Brandeisians and other antitrust figures have advocated for a more populist approach, while both Democrats and Republicans acknowledge the limitations of the consumer welfare standard.With such a diverse approach to antitrust issues, we must take a closer look at the Borkian hypothesis itself, its pitfalls and potential benefits, so that we may create a better way going forward. This chapter examines issues of consumer welfare, competitiveness, and various other key matters on antitrust.

Keywords Democrats · Republicans · Borkian antitrust · The Sherman act · Economic ideology · Small businesses · Neo-Brandeisians

A. Portuese, *The Battle for the Future of Antitrust*, Palgrave Studies in Institutions, Economics and Law, https://doi.org/10.1007/978-3-031-75794-5_1

The Chicago School of antitrust is a misnomer: Not only has there not been only one Chicago School, but also the Chicago School's most influential leader—Judge Robert H. Bork—has never been to Chicago. There are two, and not one, Chicago Schools.[1] The first Chicago School started in the 1930s with economists such as Frank Knight, Jacob Viner, and Henry Simons. They supported interventionist antitrust policy and focused on the objective of market deconcentration.[2] The second Chicago School proved to be the most influential on antitrust. Scholars such as Richard Posner and Aaron Director, embodied the second Chicago School. But no other scholar parallel Robert Bork's standing in the (second) Chicago School. After earlier writings,[3] Robert Bork wrote his most influential book—The Antitrust Paradox.[4] Bork's book has gained so much influence in academic debates, most notably in the case law, that a "Borkian antitrust" emerged.[5] Borkian antitrust rests upon the following fundamental arguments:

- Antitrust laws should promote the principle of economic efficiency, and particularly allocative efficiency in the market;
- The promotion of allocative efficiency is tantamount to preserving and enhancing consumer welfare;
- Antitrust courts and agencies should decide cases according to the consumer welfare standard;
- The Sherman Act was drafted primarily for the promotion of the consumer welfare standard;

Borkian antitrust thus elaborated a hypothesis (a) that never garnered broad consensus contrary to conventional wisdom but, quite the contrary, experienced a continuous assault (b). The assault on Borkian antitrust may currently deploy its last jab with the inexorable rise of antitrust populism (c).

[1] Bougette et al. (2015).

[2] Id.

[3] Bork (1965a, 1965b, 1966a, 1966b, 1977).

[4] Bork (1978).

[5] Brown (1987); Paul (2020).

1 The Borkian Hypothesis

Abstract

The Chicago School of antitrust, led by Judge Robert H. Bork, advocates for increased expertise in enforcement over economic ideologies. His book, titled "The Antitrust Paradox," promotes economic efficiency and consumer welfare. However, it faces criticism due to inconsistent premises and antitrust populism. Figures such as Ralph Nader call for a radical overhaul of competition regulation in America, in order to provide a more consistent regulatory framework. This subchapter examines the issues surrounding the Bokian hypothesis, and the possibility of radical change.

Robert Bork wrote The Antitrust Paradox as a reaction to the mood of his time—the popular and the Congressional mood which he described as "nihilism."[6] Bork predicted, "a new era of antitrust expansion seems likely in Congress, which is influenced by popular moods."[7] Rep. Ralph Nader led a Study Group that filed a report titled "The Closed Enterprise System," which criticizes current antitrust enforcement and calls for a radical overhaul of the regulation of competition in America. Bork considered that "Nader's essentially nihilistic attitude" contributes to the fact that "we are urged, then, by persons in and out of Congress, to throw the antitrust book at business to improve the quality of American life. One could wish that those who want to throw the book had taken the time to understand it."[8]

Consequently, Bork authored his book to understand better "law and economics" applied to antitrust issues.[9] Bork considered that antitrust issues appeared contradictory: Some antitrust solutions preserve competition while others suppress competition. This is due to inconsistent premises upon which antitrust policy develops, and it leads to a "crisis in antitrust"—"a policy at war with itself" according to Bork's subtitle.[10] With his book, Bork ambitions to convince readers and policymakers to embark on an antitrust law & economics analysis consistent with his time's

[6] Bork (1978:5).

[7] Bork (1978:5).

[8] Bork (1978:5–6).

[9] Bork (1978:5).

[10] Bork (1978:7).

broader Chicago School tenets. Bork considers that economic analysis of antitrust may bring about greater consistency, legal predictability, and enhanced economic efficiency. Against the popular and Congressional moods aiming at throwing away antitrust books and doctrines to apply antitrust in a more populist way, Bork advocated for increased expertise (i.e., the economic expertise) in antitrust enforcement over ideologies. These ideologies pervert antitrust's historical role of "tempering" laissez-faire to preserve the free market system:

> The invasion of the law by ideologies foreign to its nature is what brings antitrust to a crisis. The capture of antitrust's potent symbolism and educative power by the ideologies of statism and interventionism would be a major loss to the ideology underpinning a liberal, democratic, and capitalist social order.[11]

Bork employed two strategies to convince the reader to follow his recommendations. First, he described how current antitrust enforcement and cases are misguided, thwart competition, punish superior efficiency absent anticompetitive conduct, and are inconsistent with one another. Second, he recommended applying economic analysis for antitrust issues to achieve greater efficiency, a more stable legal environment, and ignoring the popular and Congressional moods that may erode "the intellectual and moral legitimacy of capitalism."[12] Thus, the second (normative) tenet of Bork lies in what we call the "Borkian Hypothesis." This Hypothesis is three-pronged:

(i) Congressional intent when passing the Sherman Act was to promote the welfare of consumers;
(ii) Antitrust needs to promote the principle of economic efficiency;
(iii) Economic efficiency for antitrust means the consumer welfare standard.

We now review each prong of the Borkian Hypothesis to demonstrate none of them are correct. And yet, Borkian antitrust as a pinnacle of

[11] Bork (1978:418).
[12] Bork (1978:422).

antitrust law & economics has immensely improved antitrust enforcement. This is Bork's own paradox.

(i) Congress Intended to Promote the Consumer Welfare Standard

Robert Bork perceived the Sherman Act as a mere codification of the common law on restraints of trade—particularly the common law cases discretionarily selected during the legislative debates. The common law "relevant to the Sherman Act is an artificial construct, made up for the occasion out of a careful selection of a few recent decisions from different jurisdictions, plus a liberal admixture of the senators' own policy prescriptions."[13] But the senators' "artificial construct" of the common law does not prevent Bork from concluding confidently and seminally that:

> The legislative history of the Sherman Act, the oldest and most basic of the antitrust debates, displays the clear and exclusive policy intention of promoting consumer welfare. Both in the bills introduced and, in the debates, there are a number of explicit statements that the purpose of the legislation was the protection of consumers.[14]

Contrary to Bork's assertion that "the Sherman Act was presented and debated as a consumer welfare prescription,"[15] Congress' motivations were more consistent with the economic populism rather than with economic efficiency. Bork perceived in the Sherman rooms for efficiency-justified monopoly power. The absence of per se illegality of monopoly power benefits trade associations and other small proprietors to coalesce at the expense of large corporations' ability. In other words, the fact that the Sherman Act prohibits only "unreasonable" restraints of trade, thereby suggesting a rule of reason and not a per se illegality, does not mean, as Bork inferred, that there is an efficiency rationale behind this less stringent prescription. Instead, it merely reveals the lawmakers' preference for discretion in allowing or prohibiting restraints of trade depending on the nature of the market participants restraining trade.

[13] Bork (1978:20).

[14] Bork (1978:61).

[15] Bork (1978:66).

When Bork writes that "only a consumer welfare value that, in cases of conflict, sweeps all other values before it can account for Congress' willingness to permit efficiency-based monopoly,"[16] he confused the application of the rule of reason with an efficiency rationale. Justice D. Brandeis, opposite as he can be from Bork's antitrust analysis, will be a staunch advocate of the rule of reason precisely because he wanted to be lenient with restraints of trade by trade associations, small proprietors, and other small businesses while aggressively enforcing antitrust laws against large corporations. Bork's focus on the common law rhetoric of the Sherman Act obfuscates his analysis of the underlying populism of the Sherman Act. This piece of legislation is a populist expression of the anti-bigness sentiment widely developed during the Gilded Age and widely shared across the aisles.

The legislative intent behind the Sherman Act has never been primarily the efficiency of the market—expressed via a consumer welfare prescription. Instead, it has been a distributional wealth transfer piece of legislation pro-small business and anti-bigness, irrespective of the superior efficiency of the latter. The "deceptive simplicity of the Sherman Act" fouled Bork: As Letwin argues, this simplicity "has led historians to believe that the intention of Congress was equally simple. Although they have not agreed on what the intention was, these historians have shared the view that the motives of Congress were elementary and unmixed and have differed chiefly over whether Congress was sincere."[17] The meaning of the Sherman Act remains impenetrable because it is a mixture of the influential populism to which politicians were sensitive together with a language of the common law aimed at signaling that the Sherman Act was merely a statutory provision of the current laws:

> It should not be surprising then that although the Sherman Act was passed by a virtually unanimous vote, and although its language is dismayingly clear, the administrations and courts charged with enforcing it have experienced so much difficulty in settling its meaning.[18]

[16] Bork (1978:62).

[17] Letwin (1954:53).

[18] Letwin (1954:54).

The populist mood of the time of passing the Sherman Act led Congressmen to address the public hate of trusts.[19] Contrary to Bork's assertion that the "Sherman Act was evidently designed to protect the flow of commerce and not to use commerce as a pretext for reaching other ends,"[20] the Sherman Act was explicitly intended to reduce the flow of commerce. Indeed, Senator Sherman introduced a bill not to the Senate Committee on Commerce or Judiciary—which would bolster Bork's hypothesis—but rather to the Senate Committee on Finance: The Sherman Act is essentially a tariff bill which applied to conspiracies with foreign states: The prohibition of Sect. 3 regarding conspiracies with companies in foreign states is the novelty of the Sherman Act from the common law.[21] Indeed, when introducing the bill, Senator Sherman stated:

> I did not originally intend to make any extended argument on this trust bill, because I supposed that the public facts upon which it is founded and the general necessity of some legislation were so manifest that no debate was necessary to bring those facts to the attention of the Senate [...] Unlawful combinations, unlawful at common law, now extend to all the states and interfere with our foreign and domestic commerce and with the importation and sale of goods subject to a duty under the laws of the United States, against which only the general government can secure relief. They not only affect our commerce with foreign nations, but trade and transportation among the several states. The purpose of this bill is to enable the courts of the United States to apply the same remedies against combinations which injuriously affect the interests of the United States that have been applied in the several states to protect local interest.[22]

Consequently, it is clear that the Sherman Act is a tariff bill aimed at sanctioning international combinations in the analogous way domestic combinations were outlawed (hence the support of corporate magnates who perceived the Sect. 3 of the Sherman Act as applicable against international competition), and to federalize the different State antitrust laws of which were geographically constrained. Contrary to Bork's hypothesis,

[19] Letwin (1954:55).

[20] Bork (1978:63).

[21] Letwin (1954:88).

[22] Sherman (1895:1072).

the efficiency and the interest of the consumers are very ancillary: The government's interest to levy taxes and the interest of small producers represent the primary objectives one can possibly infer from the tone of the Congressional debates.

(ii) Antitrust Needs to Promote the Principle of Economic Efficiency

Although driven by populist intents, the Sherman Act and, more generally, the antitrust laws ought to be interpreted for the efficient functioning of the competitive process. The Borkian argument of antitrust originalism is fundamentally flawed, yet its implications are not. In other words, Bork commanded us to interpret antitrust laws to promote economic efficiency because the legislative intent of Congress was presumably to promote such efficiency. Although Congress did not have such intent (at least as a primary intent), it should not lead to refraining from embracing Bork's normative claim that antitrust laws should be conducive to enhance economic efficiency. In short, regardless of Congress' intent, antitrust laws need to foster economic efficiency not for originalist reasons but for rational reasons.[23] The populist originalism of the Sherman Act needs to be disregarded to endorse an efficiency-enhancing analysis more consistent with the common law language of the Act.

Although even before Bork's work some decisions had already deviated from a per se illegality of monopoly or market power, these were exceptional rulings. Examples of these seminal cases are Standard Oil,[24] US Steel,[25] International Harvester,[26] Chicago Board of Trade,[27] Alcoa,[28] and United States v. Grinnell.[29]

In Standard Oil (1911), the United States Supreme Court stated that "[t]his country has followed the line of development of the law of England, and the public policy has been to prohibit, or treat as illegal, contracts, or acts entered into with intent to wrong the public and which

[23] Peritz (1990:269–275).

[24] Standard Oil Co. of New Jersey v. United States, 221 U.S. 1 (1911).

[25] United States v. United States Steel Corp., 251 U.S. 417 (1920).

[26] United States v. International Harvester Co., 274 U.S. 693 (1927).

[27] Chicago Board of Trade v. United States, 246 U.S. 231 (1918).

[28] United States v. Aluminum Co. of America, 148 F.2d 416 (1945).

[29] United States v. Grinnell Corp., 384 U.S. 563 (1966).

unreasonably restrict competitive conditions, limit the right of individuals, restrain the free flow of commerce, or bring about public evils such as the enhancement of prices." In the case at hand, the combination of stocks of several companies in the hands of the Standard Oil Company of New Jersey was found to constitute a combination in restraint of trade and also an attempt to monopolize and a monopolization, pursuant to Sect. 2 of the Sherman Act, considering the specific circumstances of the market and of the parties' behavior, which had acted "unreasonably." Therefore, although the case also resulted in the finding of an antitrust law infringement and led to divestitures, it adopted a different standard of analysis than the one observed in American Tobacco.

The Supreme Court understood that the unification of power and control "was the inevitable result" of the aggregation of the stocks of the corporations involved, and in the "absence of countervailing circumstances," it resulted in an unlawful act. The Supreme Court also differentiated the artificial combination of stocks from a dominancy of the industry "as a result of normal methods of industry development," and concluded that the case involved "the intent to drive other from the field, and to exclude them from their right to trade." As a result of its ruling, the Supreme Court determined the breakup of Standard Oil into several, separate companies.

In US Steel (1920), the Supreme Court stated that "[a]n industrial combination short of a monopoly is not objectionable under the act merely because of its size – its capital and power of production – or merely because of a power to restrain competition, if not exerted." In addition, in an allusion to an economic-effects approach, it held, according to testimonies, that "competition was not restrained and that prices varied or remained constant according to natural conditions" and that this fact outweighed the Government's claim that an illegal conduct had been undertaken. Therefore, the Supreme Court ruled that the Government failed to demonstrate the defendant's liability under the Sherman Act. Likewise, in International Harvester (1927), the Supreme Court acknowledged that "[t]he law does not make the mere size of a corporation, or the existence of unexerted power on its part, an offense, when unaccompanied by unlawful conduct in the exercise of its power."

The Chicago Board of Trade case, by its turn, involved a suit brought by the US government against the Chicago Board of Trade, under the claim that its "call" rule infringed the Sherman Act. According to this rule, the bids for the purchase of grains remained fixed at the day's closing bid on the call until the opening of the next session, instead of the previous regime where member fixed their bids throughout the day at the prices they saw fit. The District Court for the Northern District of Illinois ruled that the adoption and enforcement of the "call" rule was a "combination or conspiracy to restrain interstate and foreign trade and commerce."

However, the Supreme Court reversed such decision, having considered that the District Court failed to take into account the "history and purpose of the call rule," which was a "reasonable regulation of business consistent with the provisions of the Anti-Trust Law." According to the Supreme Court, the call rule "had no appreciable effect on general markets prices; nor did it materially affect the total volume of grain" commercialized in the market. In fact, the Supreme Court reasoned that the conduct resulted in pro-competitive effects that helped to improve market conditions, including the increase of market transparency and the reduction of supply uncertainties. This case is an example of Court's consideration of the effects of a purported practice, and not only of a certain conduct in itself.

In Alcoa, a lawsuit was brought claiming that the Aluminum Company of America ("Alcoa") had (i) monopolized the market for "virgin" aluminum ingot; (ii) committed a series of unlawful practices, ancillary to its monopoly; and (iii) engaged in an unlawful conspiracy with Aluminum Limited. After a decision to dismiss the complaint, the case was appealed to the Court of Appeals of the Second Circuit, which reversed such decision and condemned the defendants.

On the one hand, the case is another example of a Court's understanding that monopolies should not be deemed per se illegal. The Circuit Court of Appeals clearly reasoned that a monopoly, if found, was not per se unlawful under Sect. 2 of the Sherman Act. More importantly, this case demonstrated the need for examining the "origin of a monopoly may be critical in determining its legality." In fact, the decision cites examples of "lawful monopolies," such as a patent or a copyright. Therefore, according to this view, "size does not determine guilt" and "there must be some 'exclusion' of competitors," a "wrongful intent" or the use of "unduly coercive means" for a monopoly to be considered illegal:

> What engendered these compunctions is reasonably plain; persons may unwittingly find themselves in possession of a monopoly, automatically so to say: that is, without having intended either to put an end to existing

> competition, or to prevent *430 competition from arising when none had existed; they may become monopolists by force of accident. Since the Act makes "monopolizing" a crime, as well as a civil wrong, it would be not only unfair, but presumably contrary to the intent of Congress, to include such instances. A market may, for example, be so limited that it is impossible to produce at all and meet the cost of production except by a plant large enough to supply the whole demand. Or there may be changes in taste or in cost which drive out all but one purveyor. A single producer may be the survivor out of a group of active competitors, merely by virtue of his superior skill, foresight and industry. In such cases a strong argument can be made that, although, the result may expose the public to the evils of monopoly, the Act does not mean to condemn the resultant of those very forces which it is its prime object to foster: finis opus coronat. The successful competitor, having been urged to compete, must not be turned upon when he wins. The most extreme expression of this view is in United States v. United States Steel Corporation, 251 U.S. 417, 40 S. Ct. 293, 64 L. Ed. 343, 8 A.L.R. 1121, from which we quote in the margin;[2] and which Sanford, J., in part repeated in United States v. International Harvester Corporation, 274 U.S. 693, 708, 47 S. Ct. 748, 71 L. Ed. 1302. It so chances that in both instances the corporation had less than two-thirds of the production in its hands, and the language quoted was not necessary to the decision; so that even if it had not later been modified, it has not the authority of an actual decision. But, whatever authority it does have was modified by the gloss of Cardozo, J., in United States v. Swift & Co., 286 U.S. 106, p. 116, 52 S. Ct. 460, 463, 76 L. Ed. 999, when he said, "Mere size is not an offense against the Sherman Act unless magnified to the point at which it amounts to a monopoly but size carries with it an opportunity for abuse that is not to be ignored when the opportunity is proved to have been utilized in the past." "Alcoa's" size was "magnified" to make it a "monopoly"; indeed, it has never been anything else; and its size, not only offered it an "opportunity for abuse," but it "utilized" its size for "abuse," as can easily be shown.

On the other hand, controversially, the Court of Appeals decided that Alcoa had unlawfully attempted to monopolize the market by achieving a 90% market share and by adopting measures to outplay its rivals, including pro-competitive ones, such as expanding its productive capacity:

> It was not inevitable that it should always anticipate increases in the demand for ingot and be prepared to supply them. Nothing compelled it to keep doubling and redoubling its capacity before others entered the field. It insists that it never excluded competitors; but we can think of no

> more effective exclusion than progressively to embrace each new opportunity as it opened, and to face every newcomer with new capacity already geared into a great organization, having the advantage of experience, trade connections and the elite of personnel. Only in case we interpret "exclusion" as limited to manoeuvres not honestly industrial, but actuated solely by a desire to prevent competition, can such a course, indefatigably pursued, be deemed not "exclusionary." So to limit it would in our judgment emasculate the Act; would permit just such consolidations as it was designed to prevent.

Therefore, the Alcoa case is a controversial case, frustrating the notion of "competition on the merits." Corroborating this understanding, in another polemic aspect, the decision stated that the law acknowledged the existence of other, non-economic reasons to forbid monopolies, including "preserving the competitive position of small businesses":

> We have been speaking only of the economic reasons which forbid monopoly; but, as we have already implied, there are others, based upon the belief that great industrial consolidations are inherently undesirable, regardless of their economic results. In the debates in Congress Senator Sherman himself in the passage quoted in the margin showed that among the purposes of Congress in 1890 was a desire to put an end to great aggregations of capital because of the helplessness of the individual before them. Another aspect of the *429 same notion may be found in the language of Mr. Justice Peckham in United States v. Trans-Missouri Freight Association, supra, at page 323 (166 U.S. 290, 17 S. Ct. 540, 41 L.Ed. 1007). That Congress is still of the same mind appears in the Surplus Property Act of 1944, 50 U.S.C.A.Appendix § 1611 et seq., and the Small Business Mobilization Act, 50 U.S.C.A.Appendix § 1101 et seq. Not only does § 2(d) of the first declare it to be one aim of that statute to "preserve the competitive position of small business concerns.

In United States v. Grinnell, the Supreme Court again understood an offense to §2° has two elements: (i) the possession of monopoly power in the relevant market; and (ii) the "willful acquisition or maintenance of that power as distinguished from growth or development as a consequence of a superior product, business acumen, or historic accident." The case involved a thorough discussion of relevant market definitions. In the end, the Supreme Court concluded that Grinnell and its subsidiaries controlled over 87% of the market and, thus, had monopoly power. More importantly, the Supreme Court understood that the defendants achieved such a position through a series of acquisitions and unlawful practices, including imposing long term to clients in order to constitute significant barriers to competitors.

But if antitrust needs to promote the principle of economic efficiency for a consequentialist, and not an originalist, reason, what does the principle of economic efficiency mean? Economists commonly agree that the principle of economic efficiency encompasses three indissociable yet contradictory elements[30]:

- Allocative efficiency: resources are efficiently allocated whenever good, and services are in the hands of those who value them the most. Allocative efficiency is achieved whenever the right mix of goods and services are being produced, and in the right output level. In other words, allocative efficiency is present in a given market by producing up to the point where additional value consumers receive from a unit of output equals the cost of producing that unit of output. This transactional efficiency ensures that transaction costs are low enough for potential gains from trade to take place to attain an optimal allocation of resources in the market;
- Productive efficiency: the ratio between inputs and outputs is optimized through technical efficiency so that increased productivity will allow for more significant gains from production. Productive efficiency is achieved when a given level of output is produced at the lowest possible cost;
- Dynamic efficiency (innovation): innovation occurs when firms develop new products or new methods (e.g., different steps; different equipment) of producing goods.[31] The capacity to innovate will lead the market to generate (and adjust to) changes so that an evolutionary process ensures allocative and productive efficiencies in the longer term. A dynamically efficient economy is one in which the level of innovation maximizes long-term social welfare.

This taxonomy is not merely theoretical—it has tremendous antitrust implications.[32] Allocative and productive efficiencies look at the current

[30] Fernandes (2022).

[31] Organisation for Economic Co-operation and Development ("OECD") (2007).

[32] Nelson & Smith (2015).

situation of a certain market (static efficiencies). Dynamic efficiency, instead, reflects how decisions made today affect the future of the competitive environment in a given market (dynamic efficiencies or innovation incentives). Economists consider that the three types of efficiencies are equally important—namely, allocative, and productive efficiencies for a static perspective and dynamic efficiency for a more dynamic view of competition. In the Knightian tradition of static analysis, Bork considered that "the role of antitrust, then, lies at that stage of the economic process in which production and distribution of goods and services are organized following the scale of values that consumers choose by the relative willingness to purchase."[33] However, he explicitly overlooked dynamic efficiency (innovation) as both a source of wealth and as an objective of antitrust laws:

> These two factors may conveniently be called allocative efficiency and productive efficiency. (When, for convenience, the word "efficiency" alone is used, productive efficiency is meant.) These two types of efficiency make up the overall efficiency that determines the level of our society's wealth, or consumer welfare. The whole task of antitrust can be summed up as the effort to improve allocative efficiency without impairing productive efficiency so greatly as to produce either no gain or a net loss in consumer welfare.[34]

Therefore, Borkian antitrust is inherently static in perspective. This is problematic for two reasons. First, the source of wealth is innovation, progress, and the evolutionary process of value creation. Considering only static efficiencies ignores the impacts caused by improvements in products and services, and in production techniques over time. According to which evolutionary changes (i.e., innovation) drive economic growth, the Schumpeterian intuition proves to be tested and verified.[35] The growth of the capitalist economy resembles an "organic process" where the evolutionary changes constantly provide for the economy's dynamism. Dynamic competition acknowledges the impact of innovation which increases consumer welfare (either by offering higher quality or new products, or by offering products with newer techniques that lower costs).

[33] Bork (1978:91).

[34] Bork (1978:91).

[35] Schumpeter (1942:81–86); Solow (1956); Teece (2009:234–259); Aghion (2004).

Indeed, "the fundamental impulse that sets and keeps the capitalist engine in motion comes from the new consumers' goods, the new methods of production or transportation, the new markets, the new forms of industrial organization that capitalist enterprise creates," wrote Schumpeter.[36] And yet, this dynamic process of innovation often contradicts static considerations such as allocative and productive efficiencies: "A system –any system, economic or other – that at every given point of time fully utilizes its possibilities to the best advantage may yet, in the long run, be inferior to a system that does so at no given point of time, because the latter's failure to do so maybe a condition for the level or speed of long-run performance."[37] In other words, the imperfect competition represents the sine qua non condition of innovation: Dynamic efficiency proves more essential than other efficiencies for long-term growth and social welfare. And yet, Bork disregards the Schumpeterian intuition with a narrow focus on static efficiencies, thereby hampering long-run dynamic efficiency (innovation). Indeed, as Bork confessed, "this book will try to show that rules can be devised which reflect and resolve the tension between productive efficiency and allocative efficiency accurately enough for the law to confer a net benefit."[38]

The overall point of the Borkian concept of economic efficiency, and more precisely of the consumer welfare standard, is to reach an optimal conciliation between static efficiencies while ignoring dynamic efficiency.

Second, to ascribe to antitrust laws (and enforcers) an objective to pursue static objectives frustrates the Borkian claim that "consumer welfare, in this sense, is merely another term for the wealth of a nation."[39] The consumer welfare standard is an abridged economic growth perspective: It attempts to maximize allocative and productive efficiencies as a proxy for economic growth, whereas the growth inherently comes from dynamic efficiency (innovation). This is Bork's paradox: The Antitrust Paradox provides a seminal analysis of antitrust and advocates for economic efficiency in enforcing antitrust laws. But, the primary source of efficiency remains overlooked by the author. Bork lamented over a "policy

[36] Schumpeter (1942:83).

[37] Id.

[38] Bork (1978:129).

[39] Bork (1978:90).

at war with itself." Still, his prescriptions remain within another fundamental contradiction: In a static competition model, antitrust enforcers can infer from prices above a "perfectly competitive price" a pricing policy at odds with the consumer welfare standard since the traditional approach Bork attacks can infer that these prices reveal anticompetitive conduct. To paraphrase Bork, Bork's conception of efficiency is a model at war with itself.

In both approaches, imperfect competition may lead to sanctions of the dominant firm. To be sure, "Bork's The Antitrust Paradox was an 'old economy' book, however, taking very little notice of intellectual property rights, networks, and other recent technologies..." (Hovenkamp 2018:603). Indeed, the source of competition lies in innovative, technology-intensive products, services, and arrangements. It thus appears necessary to depart from Bork's Antitrust Paradox as a guide for today's disruptive economy, albeit Bork's valuable insights on effect-based antitrust shall certainly serve as practical antitrust analysis. The consumer welfare standard remains a proxy for an abridged principle of economic efficiency where its main component—dynamic efficiency—is absent.

(iii) Economic Efficiency for Antitrust Means the Consumer Welfare Standard

Departing from a world where concentration was necessarily seen as an evil to be fought, Bork's ideas of market efficiently certainly contributed at the time to cast doubt on the Brandeisian paradigm. For these reasons, Borkian antitrust has dramatically influenced antitrust law & economics in general and antitrust enforcement in particular. Several cases illustrate that.

In General Dynamics[40] (1974), the District Court for the Northern District of Illinois rejected the action brought by the Government aiming to block the acquisition of United Electric Coal Companies, a strip-mining coal producer, by General Dynamics Corporation, a deep mining coal producer. To prove its claim that the merger would substantially lessen competition in the market for the production and sale of coal, the Government presented past production statistics showing an alleged increase in market concentration, and that the merger would increase

[40] United States v. General Dynamics Corp., 415 U.S. 486 (1974).

the merged entity's market share, contributing to such trend toward concentration. However, by upholding the District Court's decision, the Supreme Court invoked an economic-effects approach, claiming that relying solely on market share data did not prove a substantial lessening of competition in the relevant markets:

> While the Government's statistical showing might have been sufficient to support a finding of "undue concentration" in the absence of other considerations, the District Court was justified in finding that other pertinent factors affecting the coal industry and appellees' business mandated a conclusion that no substantial lessening of competition occurred or was threatened by the acquisition. Ample evidence showed that United Electric does not have sufficient reserves, which are a key factor in measuring a coal producer's market strength, to make it a significant competitive force. Thus, in terms of probable future ability to compete, rather than in terms of past production on which the Government relied, the court was warranted in concluding that the merger did not violate § 7 of the Act. Pp. 415 U. S. 494-504.

In Marine Bancorporation[41] (1974), the US Government challenged the merger whereby Marine Bancorporation, Inc., (through its subsidiary, the National Bank of Commerce), proposed to acquire the Washington Trust Bank. The case discussed the concept of potential competition, related to the possibility that the target company was a potential entrant in the geographic market (Spokane, Washington) and, thus, it exerted competitive pressure on the incumbents, including the acquiring company. The Supreme Court upheld the decision of the District Court for the Western District of Washington that had rejected the Government's plea. According to the courts, the Government had failed to meet its burden of proof that the merger would violate § 7 of the Clayton Act, having considered that the existence of significant entry barriers demonstrated entry was not viable through other means. More importantly, as in General Dynamics, the courts rejected the Government's narrative that the market was concentrated according solely to its structure (market shares):

[41] United States v. Marine Bancorporation, Inc., 418 U.S. 602 (1974).

> In an effort to establish that the Spokane commercial banking market is oligopolistic, the Government relied primarily on concentration ratios indicating that three banking organizations (including WTB) control approximately 92% of total deposits in Spokane. The District Court held against the Government on this point, finding that "a highly competitive market" existed which "does not suffer from parallel or other anticompetitive practices attributable to undue market power." 1971 Trade Cas. 74,496, p. 94,246. The court apparently gave great weight to the testimony of the banks' expert witnesses concerning the number of bank organizations and banking offices operating in the Spokane metropolitan area. The record indicates that neither the Government nor the appellees undertook any significant study of the performance, as compared to the structure, of the commercial banking market in Spokane.

In *Cargill v. Monfort*[42] (1986), Monfort of Colorado, Inc., brought an action under § 16 of the Clayton Act to enjoin Cargill's acquisition (through Excel Corporation, its subsidiary) of Spencer Beef. The Supreme Court rejected Monfort's claim that the merger would "impair its ability to compete due to a concentration of economic power," given the perspective that the merged entity would be in a position to cut prices offered to consumers. Instead, the Supreme Court posited that price competition was a signal of the vigorous competition that the antitrust laws aimed to protect:

> The kind of competition that Monfort alleges here, competition for increased market share, is not activity forbidden by the antitrust laws. It is simply, as petitioners claim, vigorous competition. To hold that the antitrust laws protect competitors from the loss of profits due to such price competition would, in effect, render illegal any decision by a firm to cut prices in order to increase market share. The antitrust laws require no such perverse result, for "[i]t is in the interest of competition to permit dominant firms to engage in vigorous competition, including price competition.

Nevertheless, Borkian antitrust has also experienced constant criticisms. Using a misnomer, Bork ascribed to the consumer welfare standard to maximize both consumer surplus and producer surplus. Transcribing

[42] Cargill v. Monfort, 479 U.S. 104 (1986).

theoretical economic models of perfect competition into a legal and judicially administrable standard—i.e., the consumer welfare standard—Bork considers that the consumer welfare standard suggests a balancing exercise between the consumer surplus and the producer surplus so that the social net surplus needs to be negative before prohibiting specific conduct. But, whenever the said social surplus is negative, per se rules of illegality are entirely legitimate—e.g., the reasonable-price test for judging the legality of cartels. Bork thus wrote that "the suggested reasonable-price test was in actuality an invitation to mediate between the interest of consumers in competitive prices and the interest of producers in monopoly prices. The courts, presumably, were to choose a price somewhere in between. In framing a rule of per se illegality, the courts necessarily opted for a wide consumer welfare stance."[43]

The consumer welfare standard allegedly represents an external, objective criterion for antitrust purposes. Thus, antitrust enforcers can assess the merits of a firm's conduct, irrespective of its internal functioning, rationale, and business model. However, Borkian antitrust remains external to the firm—quite opposed to a dynamic approach resting upon analyzing the firm's dynamic capabilities to appraise the competitiveness of its conduct.[44] Indeed, Borkian antitrust explicitly disparaged the firm's viewpoint despite appraising its competitive conduct:

> In antitrust the required common denominator is provided by the goal or value of consumer welfare. In a system which permits consumers to define their own welfare by their purchases, it follows, that, with an important reservation to be mentioned shortly, a firm's efficiency is shown by its success. It is useless, for antitrust purposes, to study the minimum efficient size of the firm by studying the engineering efficiencies of the plant and production line because the important factor is consumer response to what comes off the production line.[45]

The consumer welfare standard is a model according to which the theoretical triangle of the consumer surplus (and the producer surplus)

[43] Bork (1978:73).

[44] Teece (2009).

[45] Bork (1978:105–106).

needs to shrink to justify antitrust interventions.[46] The Borkian "consumer welfare prescription"[47] fits into a perfect competition model whereby any price charged at a supra-competitive price will generate a dead-weight loss, thereby shrinking the consumer surplus and the overall economic efficiency. Bork was, however, well aware of the consumer welfare standard's limitations—he knew it did not consider a dynamic view of the competitive process by focusing on static efficiencies and inferring ill-suited implications. Indeed, he confessed that:

> Perhaps this representation of the consumer welfare model contains too many traps for the unwary, but I have adopted it because it illustrates so clearly the relationship between allocative and productive efficiencies in determining consumer wealth. It makes plain the error committed by the Supreme Court in holding either that efficiency is irrelevant or that it is actually a reason to strike down a merger.[48]

However inaccurate, the consumer welfare standard is instrumental in shifting antitrust enforcement toward an efficient (albeit abridged) view of antitrust. The consumer welfare standard lies on Oliver Williamson's model of the dead-weight loss generated by mergers.[49] Unfortunately, Williamson's mathematical model is a theoretical one with little practicalities. Indeed, Bork acknowledged that Williamson sees his model as a "naïve model," and yet, rejects Williamson's qualifications of his model to build the consumer welfare standard and infer antitrust implications:

> Williamson refers to his diagram as a 'naïve model' and suggests a number of possible qualifications. Some relate to the elements of efficiency and the method of weighing the two kinds of efficiency...Each of these qualifications should be rejected, and antitrust should concern itself solely with allocative and productive efficiency. This is a subject closely related to the goals of antitrust policy....[50]

[46] Bork (1978:107–110).

[47] Reiter v. Sonotone Corp., 442 U.S. 330, 343 (1979).

[48] Bork (1978:109).

[49] Bork (1978:107–115).

[50] Bork (1978:109).

The lack of practicality of the theoretical model, upon which the consumer welfare standard rests, undermines its normativity. It induces a price-centric antitrust model at the expense of innovation-centric antitrust enforcement.[51] In this sense, both Williamson's dead-weight loss model and Borkian antitrust have the fragility of neglecting non-price factors in competition assessment. Imperfect competition shows that, in most markets, firms compete on product differentiation, including quality, design, and innovation. The more a firm can distinguish its products from the ones of competitors, the lower its elasticity of demand and its temporary market power. Anyhow, such market power can only be sustained if the company is able to continually differentiate itself from its rivals.

Borkian antitrust explicitly discounts technological innovation as "progressiveness": He both asserts that such progressiveness is part of the consumer welfare standard while stating that there is "a more fundamental difficulty with the notion of counting progressiveness as a goal of policy: it is not clear how much progressiveness is desirable."[52] It appears illogical to simultaneously state that "progressiveness" (i.e., technological progress/innovation) is part of the consumer welfare standard. Still, it remains supposedly unclear how much antitrust enforcers should desire it. If it is part of the consumer welfare standard, then it should be maximized since it is allegedly maximized in the welfare maximization model that Bork uses.

It is unclear how much technological progress one may want, according to Bork, only because this suggests an implicit confession that such progressiveness needs to be weighed out against static efficiencies. Indeed, as technological progress suggests dynamic efficiency, Bork acknowledged in passing that the tension between static efficiencies and dynamic efficiency is real, yet not scrutinized in The Antitrust Paradox.

2 The Continuous Assault

Abstract

The Borkian account of antitrust legislative history is seen as erroneous as it artificially incorporated modern economic theories into the 1890

[51] Gilbert (2020).

[52] Bork (1978:132).

Sherman Act. In fact, the Sherman Act was a response to disruptive innovations of the Golden Age, where larger corporations competed against small proprietors with more efficient and innovative capabilities. The Act was likely passed at the behest of small businesses, injured by a technological revolution that left them on the sidelines. Lande's critique of the Antitrust Paradox proved to be lasting, as it pointed out the essence of the consumer welfare standard, demonstrating that Congress passed antitrust laws to further economic objectives, primarily preventing unfair transfers of wealth from consumers to firms with market power. Debunking the Borkian legislative account is equivalent to debunking the Borkian prescription, which represents a fundamental strategic mistake made by Bork. Critics have pointed out that Borkian antitrust relied on unrealistic assumptions, such as perfect competition and market rivalry, which should not be accepted without unnecessary controversy.

The Borkian account of the antitrust legislative history is erroneous because it artificially put modern and complex economic theories into the mouth of the lawmakers of the 1890 Sherman Act. Described as "unhelpful,"[53] Bork's historical account of the Sherman Act suffers from the author's desire to instill "neoclassical economic values espoused by the Chicago School's antitrust policy [in] what the framers of the Sherman Act had in mind."[54] It does not work; it should not work.

The Sherman Act's populist origins—as both a deconcentrationist and a wealth-transfer tool from large corporations and consumers to small businesses—are and should be accepted without unnecessary controversy.[55] Antitrust originalism is no argument for antitrust economics and is no excuse to bend an accurate account of the legislative history. The Sherman Act is a (protectionist) reaction to disruptive innovations of the Golden Age where larger corporations outcompeted small proprietors with more efficient and more innovative capabilities. This understanding motivated the decisions in American Tobacco,[56] DuPont,[57] and Lehigh Valley,[58] as described previously.

[53] Hovenkamp (2005:39).

[54] Id.

[55] Hart (2001).

[56] United States v. American Tobacco Co., 221 U.S. 106 (1911).

[57] United States v. E. I. Du Pont De Nemours & Co., 188 F. 127 (3d Cir. 1911).

[58] United States v. Lehigh Valley R.R., 254 U.S. 255 (1920).

Indeed, as Baker sums up, "old ways of life were swept aside. Many farmers, workers, families, and small businesses felt powerless to fend off exploitation by seemingly artificial concentrations of economic power. In response, Congress passed the Sherman Antitrust Act."[59] It is thus clear that the "Sherman Act was very likely passed at the behest of small businesses, injured by a technological revolution that left them on the sidelines."[60]

More fundamentally, Borkian antitrust in particular, and the Chicago school of antitrust law & economics, experienced constant criticisms before releasing the Antitrust Paradox[61],and even more so after its release.[62] Although the Chicago School influence culminated in the 2000s, Borkian antitrust soon after The Antitrust Paradox experienced persistent critiques.[63] While in 1990, Peritz vilified "Bork's implausible and inaccurate account of the Sherman Act's passage,"[64] Lande's reception of The Antitrust Paradox provided a lasting critique of the essence of the consumer welfare standard.[65] Lande powerfully demonstrated that "Congress passed the antitrust laws to further economic objectives, but primarily objectives of a distributive rather than of an efficiency nature. In other words, Congress was concerned principally with preventing 'unfair' transfers of wealth from consumers to firms with market power."[66]

But, since Bork has tied up his advocacy for the consumer welfare standard with the originalist argument (i.e., antitrust law should maximize consumer welfare because Congress so wanted when passing the Sherman Act), debunking the Borkian legislative account is equivalent to debunking the Borkian prescription—namely, the consumer welfare prescription. This represents a fundamental (strategic) mistake made by Bork from which his adversaries will astutely benefit. The normative implications become equally inaccurate once the legislative interpretation

[59] Baker (2019:36).

[60] Hovenkamp (2005:42).

[61] Flynn (1977).

[62] Lande (1982;1999).

[63] Crane (2014).

[64] Peritz (1990:282).

[65] Lande (1982).

[66] Lande (1982:68).

proves inaccurate, Lande and others would eloquently argue.[67] Indeed, Lande's article of 1982 paved the way for, in his own words, "a post-Chicago antitrust renaissance" where antitrust laws do not contribute to efficiency but, more importantly, to wealth transfers from large corporations to consumers (and small businesses).[68] Accurately anticipating that the Chicago school's flawed basic premises will one day cause its crepuscule, Hovenkamp explained that Borkian antitrust relied on unrealistic assumptions.[69]

Numerous critics quickly pinpointed these unrealistic assumptions after the publication of The Antitrust Paradox. For instance, Jack High relevantly suggested that while "Bork rejects both perfect competition and market rivalry," in fact, "when we turn to Bork's analysis, we find that perfect competition and market rivalry both figure prominently. Perfect competition is used to derive a standard of allocational efficiency."[70] This undue reliance on the perfect competition model contradicts the firms' necessity to compete and innovate—what Schumpeter's described as the process of "creative destruction." This process clashes with the model of perfect competition Schumpeter wrote:

> If we try to visualize how perfect competition works or would work in the process of creative destruction, we arrive at a still more discouraging result. This will not surprise use, considering that all the essential facts of that process are absent from the general schema of economic life that yields the traditional propositions about perfect competition.[71]

The Borkian's overlook of dynamic competition results in the theory of market rivalry whereby imperfect knowledge in the market creates the very profit opportunities which lay at the core of the innovation incentives of entrepreneurs because "market rivalry, in essence, is competition for profit."[72] The tension between the dynamic view of competition and Borkian's static view of competition proves considerable implications

[67] Lande (1999).

[68] Lande (1999:967).

[69] Hovenkamp (1985).

[70] High (1984).

[71] Schumpeter (1942:104).

[72] High (1984).

whenever we reflect on the entrepreneur's motives to introduce a new product. Indeed, "in the dynamic view, the successful introduction of a new product increases both productive and allocative efficiency. There is no conflict or trade-off. Under static assumptions, there is no need to discover new or better techniques; they are already known."[73] Therefore, a price increase or output decrease under static competition models necessarily amounts to anticompetitive conduct and cannot build up the necessary capabilities for product innovation.[74]

Borkian antitrust experienced continuous assaults with different schools of thought. First, the Harvard School, representing the structural approach Bork chastised in his book, predictably fired back.[75] Second, the Brandeisian School remained somehow vocal, albeit much lesser than its revived cousin nowadays—the Neo-Brandeisians.[76] Third, the Austrian school vilipended Bork's emphasis on economic efficiency and allegedly measurable costs and benefits in the neoclassical tradition.[77] Fourth, the so-called post-Chicago school provided a qualification, minor yet non-inconsequential, of Borkian antitrust.[78] These approaches provided continuous streams of criticisms and qualification of Bork's emphasis on the consumer welfare standard.

Because of its inherent weaknesses, the Chicago School "was vulnerable."[79] As its poster child, Borkian antitrust remained vulnerable. The recent, most vigorous attacks expressed by antitrust populists further exacerbate such vulnerability.

3 The Seemingly Last Assault

Abstract

Critics of Borkian antitrust, particularly Neo-Brandeisians, have advocated for a more populist approach. Barry Lynn and Lina Khan, both

[73] Id.

[74] Barney (2001); Teece (2009).

[75] Kovacic (2007); Fox (1981); Areeda & Turner (1978).

[76] Pitofsky (1979); Lande (1982); Page (1991).

[77] Block (1977,1994); DiLorenzo & High (1988); Boudreaux & DiLorenzo (1993).

[78] Baker (1989); Sullivan (1995); Hovenkamp (2001); Evans & Padilla (2005); Dibadj (2004).

[79] Hovenkamp (2001:268).

prominent antitrust figures, have called for a shift away from Borkian antitrust. Both Democrats and Republicans have acknowledged the limitations of the consumer welfare standard and advocated for more vigorous antitrust enforcement to combat economic concentration. The future of Borkian antitrust is uncertain, as populist attacks on its principles grow stronger. The New Brandeisian Movement has successfully challenged the status quo, paving the way for a new era of antitrust enforcement.

Any proclamation of the death of Borkian antitrust as illustrating the Chicago school would be "premature."[80] However, the intensity of the critique against Borkian antitrust is best illustrated when such an attack comes from those who may think to be its supporters. For example, Kishi wrote in The American Conservative that:

> Whereas prior generations of lawmakers protected the American citizenry as businessmen, entrepreneurs, and growers, Bork led a revolution that sacrificed the small producer at the altar of efficiency and cheap goods. With the publication of The Antitrust Paradox 40 years ago, the American citizen was, in a very real sense, reduced to a mere consumer.[81]

However original and direct, these attacks on Borkian antitrust can arise from conservative perspectives. The most vocal and impactful attacks come from the Neo-Brandeisians. They achieved to formulate influential critics who entered mainstream views about antitrust. A revived criticism of Borkian antitrust surfaced in the late 2000s.[82] The decade of the 2010s started with an influential outburst of the populist, Neo-Brandeisian critiques of Borkian antitrust. For instance, Barry Lynn, then director at New America and later founder of the influential Open Markets Institute, wrote in March 2010 a call for antitrust to re-discover its deconcentrationist objective.[83] Warning against the risks of consolidation in a Brandeisian language, Lynn chastised Borkian antitrust:

> The reason to promote efficiency, Bork wrote, was to increase the "welfare" of the consumer. The basic argument was as simple as it was subversive: given that consumers benefit from lower prices, and given that

[80] Crane (2019).

[81] Kishi (2018).

[82] Kirkwood & Lande (2008); Grandy (2009); Stucke (2009); Orbach (2010).

[83] Hart (2001).

> greater scale and scope gives managers the power to drive down prices, we should embrace concentration rather than resist it [...] Our first step must be to repopulate our discussions of political economics with the voices of the people who actually make our economy go. After all, real entrepreneurs and real scientists and real executives and real bankers and real farmers and real software engineers and real venture capitalists tend to understand quite well how real power is used against them.[84]

Claiming to represent the "real" people, Barry Lynn will relentlessly advocate moving away from Borkian antitrust to favor a more populist approach.[85] He will be instrumental in the publication, in 2017, of Amazon Antitrust Paradox by Lina Khan.[86] Then Legal Director of Barry Lynn's Open Markets Institute, Lina Khan, has since then become a co-author of the House Report on Big Tech and Federal Trade Commissioner. Her idea to undo Borkian antitrust to return to the Brandeisian view has become so influential that any return to Borkian antitrust now seems improbable: The populist assault on Borkian antitrust may seemingly be the last one. Indeed, a bipartisan consensus developed over the need to depart from Borkian antitrust and re-discover a more populist approach to large companies.

First, the Congressional Democrats issued in July 2017 a "Better Deal: Cracking Down on Corporate Monopolies and the Abuse of Economic and Political Power"—a manifesto that acknowledged antitrust's flawed focus on the consumer welfare standard and that advocated for a more vigorous deconcentration effort of the economy.[87] Second, the Republicans, following former President Trump's antitrust populism, embraced the ongoing techlash whereby the consumer welfare standard enabled large tech companies to thrive without sufficient checks.[88] This bipartisan consensus also materialized in the House Report on Big Tech, signed by Democrats only. Still, Republicans reach essentially the same conclusions: Borkian antitrust has unduly led to antitrust under-enforcement, and a more political view of antitrust should lead to market deconcentration.[89]

[84] Lynn (2010b).

[85] Lynn (2010a, 2012).

[86] Khan (2017).

[87] Goldfrein & Keyte (2017); Foran (2017); Stein (2017).

[88] Shapiro (2018); Hawley (2021).

[89] Nadler & Cicilline (2020); Buck (2020).

Thus, for instance, the Republicans have buried the Borkian consumer welfare standard when they write:

> The shorthand for these antitrust standards is consumer welfare, meaning that antitrust should generally only concern itself with price increases and output reductions. The challenge in Big Tech markets is that competition is mostly driven not by price or output but rather by potential innovation and forward-looking competition reviews. In many cases, this comes not from the Big Tech platforms but from startups, many of whom have been driven out of business or acquired by Big Tech. With its laser-like focus on price and output, modern antitrust appears to have missed the marketplace realities in Big Tech markets.[90]

The Congressional Republicans' stance is particularly well-aligned with the Congressional Democrats' stance when they write:

> By adopting a narrow construction of 'consumer welfare' as the sole goal of the antitrust laws, the Supreme Court has limited the analysis of competitive harm to focus primarily on price and output rather than that competitive process–contravening legislative history and legislative intent. Simultaneously, courts have adopted the view that underenforcement of the antitrust laws is preferable to overenforcement, a position at odds with the clear legislative intent of the antitrust laws, as well as the view of Congress that private monopolies are a 'menace to republican institutions.'[91]

Borkian antitrust is over: It lost in the popular press, was defeated in Congress, and soon will be displaced in courts. Such fatal assault would not have been possible without the New Brandeisian Movement—the self-proclaimed antitrust populists "with a brain."[92]

[90] Buck (2020:10).

[91] Nadler & Cicilline (2020:391).

[92] Lynn (2016).

CHAPTER 2

Brandeisian Antitrust Under Spotlights

Abstract The New Brandeis Movement, a response to the rise of multinational corporations and accelerated innovation, advocates for regulated competition to limit its pitfalls, and protect consumers and small businesses. Neo-Brandeisians, most commonly found in Europe, favor a precautionary approach to safeguard competition and democratic values. Critics of monopolies overlook the potential benefits of capitalism, while Neo-Brandeisianism advocates for a return to antitrust enforcement without considering economic analysis. The present chapter showcases each Movement's way of looking at antitrust and the economy, ultimately arguing that the balance between efficiency and societal welfare should be prioritized in shaping antitrust policy for the future.

Keywords New Brandeis movement · Antitrust laws · Innovation · Competition · Firms · FTC Act · Monopoly regulation · Precautionary approach · Over-regulation · Courts · Public sentiment · Ordoliberalism

As a reaction to Borkian antitrust and large multinational corporations rising under a quest for innovation in a highly competitive world, antitrust has recently got enamored with the old ideas of Justice Louis D. Brandeis. Portrayed as the "champion of small business" and a fierce opponent to

A. Portuese, *The Battle for the Future of Antitrust*, Palgrave Studies in Institutions, Economics and Law, https://doi.org/10.1007/978-3-031-75794-5_2

the scale economies enjoyed by large corporations, Brandeis was instrumental in passing the Federal Trade Commission Act and the Clayton Act of 1914. His idea was to regulate competition so that large, efficient, and innovative companies would limit their cut-throat competition against smaller traders and independent proprietors. In an idealized market economy where smallness prevails over efficiency and innovation, Brandeis advocated relentlessly and influentially for the protection of competitors, frequently at the expense of the process of competing via innovation.[1] The so-called "New Brandeis Movement" populates scholars and advocates with claims detached from the lessons, teachings, and better understanding we gained thanks to the antitrust law & economics over the last decades. Werden neatly captures the idealized period Brandeisians refer to. Unfortunately, such time is, and should remain, passé:

> But the New Brandeis Movement is nostalgia without memory. No one in the movement can remember Neil Armstrong walking on the moon, much less antitrust enforcement under the Assistant Attorneys General from Thurman W. Arnold to Richard J. McLaren (1938-72). Claims the Movement makes about enforcement in the old days are under-researched and over-romanticized.[2]

Neo-Brandeisians argue that they wish to preserve the competitive process rather than the mere consumer welfare standard.[3] However, their view of protecting the competitive process does not lie in protecting the capabilities and incentives which enable companies to compete for innovation or to innovate for competition.[4] They instead see the protection of the competitive process as the protection of the number of rivals on the market, leading to the misguided conclusion that less efficient, less innovative firms may need to be legally protected under antitrust laws. Indeed, "Lina Khan's notion of protecting the competitive process is active deconcentration rather than aggressive antitrust enforcement."[5] Indeed, Brandeisian antitrust is no longer antitrust–namely, sanctioning anticompetitive conduct. It is more about regulating how firms compete

[1] Portuese (2022); Portuese (2020).

[2] Werden (2020:359).

[3] Khan (2017:739).

[4] Teece (2009); Barney (2001).

[5] Werden (2020:360).

by forcing enhanced competition for some (i.e., smaller, left behind rivals) and lessening competition for others (i.e., market leaders outcompeting rivals thanks to unparalleled advantages of innovation and efficiency). This view fundamentally contests the historical role of antitrust laws. Traditionally, "antitrust protects the competitive process from private attempts to undermine it, but antitrust never actively operates to make markets more competitive."[6]

Brandeisians want to force allegedly more competition through more deconcentration. The fundamental assumption lies in the belief that the greater the number of firms of equal size in the market, the better for competition, innovation, and a wide range of social interests (such as workers, stakeholders, social and environmental goals but also race, gender, and equality objectives). Although unsubstantiated, Brandeisians' assumption embeds three fundamental implications for the characteristics antitrust currently embraces in the move away from Borkian antitrust in favor of a Brandeisian antitrust. The three fundamental tenets of Brandeisian antitrust are:

(i) *Populist antitrust*: The belief that antitrust laws should pursue a range of socio-political goals may not be limited to the consumer welfare standard. The Brandeisians' protection of the competitive process means something quite different from the traditional protection of the competitive process: It inherently refers to a deconcentrationist tool which would dismember big business for the sake of scale diseconomies and a level of competition deemed more accessible to everyone. In addition to economic factors, populists understand antitrust policy should follow other values and focus on other goals, including fighting corporate power, tackling inequality, and protecting democracy;

(ii) *Precautionary antitrust*: The regulation of competition suggests that the judicial process is ill-suited to enforce antitrust laws. The judicial process' length and uncertainty allegedly contradict the need for supervised, daily monitored regulation of competition. Antitrust requires evidence of (consumer) harm; Brandeisians' anti-monopoly vision merely requires regulation absent the need to reach evidentiary standards of harm. Although criticism on

[6] Werden (2020:360).

the courts' ability to properly intervene on antitrust issues is not exclusive from Brandeisians—the Chicago School was also skeptical about it—, Brandeisians go beyond in their critics to advocate for more rules and more prior regulation.[7] Brandeisians operate a paradigm shift from ex-post antitrust rules (i.e., antitrust liability invoked in courts) toward an ex-ante antimonopoly regulation (i.e., regulatory compliance administratively monitored). The precautionary logic—namely, intervene before hypothetical harm may occur—enters antitrust with the Brandeisians: They advocate preventive interventions despite tangible risks of stifling innovation and disruption at the expense of consumers.

(iii) *Popular antitrust*: Brandeisians disparage the role of economists, experts, and, more generally, the economic analysis of antitrust laws. Keen to take antitrust away from the courts (filled with experts engaging in the rational decision-making process), Brandeisians altogether wish to leave fewer rooms to experts, economic arguments, and deliberative discussions. For Brandeisians, antitrust is political, and politicians should impose their political agenda and preferences on the fate of specific companies. For Brandeisians, antitrust relates to values not related to economic efficiency, such as social justice, income redistribution, and de-mobilization of private power. As Brandeis was "the people's lawyer," Brandeisians want antitrust to become "the people's law."

We now scrutinize each of these facets of Brandeisian antitrust.

1 Populist Antitrust

Abstract

The New Brandeis Movement, a response to the rise of multinational corporations and innovation, advocates for regulating competition to limit its cut-throat nature. Followers of populist antitrust believe antitrust laws should pursue socio-political goals beyond consumer welfare standards. However, they also argue that protection should not include capabilities for innovation, leading to misguided conclusions about less efficient firms needing legal protection.

[7] Jacobs (1995).

Populism has no unanimous definition, and studies have given it different meanings along history. Anyhow, more important for the purposes of this book is to focus on the foundations of populism more relevant to antitrust policy. Generally, populism is usually associated with the existence of two antagonic groups, "the people" and "the elite."[8] We adopt, as often done by the American antitrust literature, the understanding that populism is associated with a fear of large corporations and sympathy for deconcentrated markets.[9]

Antitrust populism derives from the very populist origins of the Sherman Act in 1890.[10] The historical context of the passage of the Sherman Act with the creation of the People's Party ("the Populists") and, before this Party, the significant development of a wide range of grassroots populist movements (Alliancemen, Greenbackers, Anti-monopoly Party, ...) led to engrain the populist vision of competition into the first federal statute on antitrust. With the Sherman Silver Purchase Act, the Sherman Antitrust Act is one of the legislation that becomes imperative due to the popular request to reduce the aggressive competition exerted by large and technologically capable corporations. Thus, antitrust populism has long been an underlying force in enforcing the Sherman Act.[11]

Brandeis captured and operationalized the antitrust populism of the Golden Age to engrain it into the significant acts of 1914 (i.e., FTC and Clayton Acts) and the antitrust agencies' analysis. Some remarkable cases, including Trans-Missouri Freight,[12] Northern Securities Company,[13] American Tobacco,[14] DuPont,[15] and Lehigh Valley,[16] are among the ones that help explain this populist approach.

[8] Bernatt (2022).

[9] Id.

[10] Portuese (2022).

[11] Orbach (2017); Vaheesan (2014); Shapiro (2018).

[12] United States v. Trans-Missouri Freight Ass'n, 166 U.S. 290 (1897).

[13] Northern Securities Co. v. United States, 193 U.S. 197 (1904).

[14] United States v. American Tobacco Co., 221 U.S. 106 (1911).

[15] United States v. E. I. Du Pont De Nemours & Co., 188 F. 127 (3d Cir. 1911).

[16] United States v. Lehigh Valley R.R., 254 U.S. 255 (1920).

In the first case, the US Supreme Court held that an association founded by certain railway companies (the Trans-Missouri Freight Association) was illegal, pursuant to the Sherman Act. According to the decision, such statute applies "to all contracts in restraint of interstate or foreign trade or commerce without exception or limitation, and are not confined to those in which the restraint is unreasonable." In the case at hand, the Supreme Court posited that "the Government [plaintiff] is not obliged to show that the agreement in question was entered into for the purpose of restraining trade or commerce if such restraint is its necessary effect" and rejected the defendants' claim in this regard.

In Northern Securities Company (1904), the US Supreme Court banned the combination of the Great Northern and Northern Pacific Railway corporations into the Northern Securities Company, a company formed with the purpose of owning the stocks of the two previously competing railway corporations, having found that "[t]his combination is, within the meaning of the act, a 'trust;' but if not, it is a combination in restraint of interstate and international commerce, and that is enough to bring it under the condemnation of the [Sherman] act." The case is considered to be one of the emblematic "trust-buster" episodes of Theodore Roosevelt's Administration,[17] whereby the Supreme Court decided that "every combination or conspiracy which would extinguish competition between otherwise competing railroads engaged in interstate trade or commerce, and which would in that way restrain such trade or commerce, is made illegal by the act."

In American Tobacco (1911), the Supreme Court ordered the American Tobacco company to be split into four independent, competing companies, concluding that "[i]n this case, the combination, in and of itself, and also all of its constituent elements, are decreed to be illegal." Reflecting on the scope of the Sherman Act, the Supreme Court considered that a more comprehensive interpretation of such statute was needed, undermining the understanding adopted in Standard Oil that a lack of reasonability was required for a practice to be considered unlawful:

> This follows because, although it was held in the Standard Oil case that, giving to the statute a reasonable construction, the words 'restraint of trade' did not embrace all those normal and usual contracts essential to individual freedom, and the right to make which was necessary in order

[17] Kovacic (1989).

that the course of trade might be free, yet, as a result of the reasonable construction which was affixed to the statute, it was pointed out that the generic designation of the first and second sections of the law, when taken together, embraced every conceivable act which could possibly come within the spirit or purpose of the prohibitions of the law, without regard to the garb in which such acts were clothed.

In DuPont (1911), the Third Circuit Court reinforced the idea that the Sherman Act was aimed to protect "weaker competitors" against the powers of big corporations:

While all this is true, the recent decisions of the Supreme Court make it equally clear that a combination cannot escape the condemnation of the anti-trust act merely by the form it assumes or by the dress it wears. It matters not whether the combination be "in the form of a trust or otherwise," whether it be in the form of a trade association or a corporation, if it arbitrarily uses its power to force weaker competitors out of business, or to coerce them into a sale to or union with the combination, it puts a restraint upon interstate commerce, and monopolizes or attempts to monopolize a part of that commerce, in a sense that violates the anti-trust act.

Similarly, the Supreme Court found violations of the First and Second Sections of the Sherman Act and ordered divestitures in Lehigh Valley (1920), regarding the commerce of anthracite coal. Indeed, Brandeis' view of regulated competition made of small units is grounded in the "civic humanism [of] founders and the antimonopolism voiced by radical Jacksonians, Populists, Knights of Labor, and Greenbackers."[18] Thus, populism has a long tradition in American economic policy. And, like Bork's, Brandeis' views continued to influence other schools of thoughts and courts.

In the 60s, other controversial decisions were taken corroborating the lack of emphasis on economic effects, such as the blocks of the Brown Shoe,[19] Pabst Brewing,[20] and Von's Grocery[21] mergers. In Brown Shoe, the Supreme Court enjoined the merger between G. R. Kinney Company,

[18] Berk (1994:14).

[19] Brown Shoe Co., Inc. v. United States, 370 U.S. 294 (1962).

[20] United States v. Pabst Brewing Co., 384 U.S. 546 (1966).

[21] United States v. Von's Grocery Co., 384 U.S. 270 (1966).

Inc. (retailer of shoes) and the Brown Shoe Company, Inc. (manufacturer that sold shoes via retailers but also directly to consumers), which involved both vertical and horizontal effects. In this emblematic case, the Supreme Court pondered that "Congress provided no definite quantitative or qualitative tests by which enforcement agencies were to gauge the effects of a given merger." In this sense, it proposed different criteria for assessing whether a merger would "substantially lessen competition" or "tend to create a monopoly," including: (i) the size of the share of the market foreclosed; (ii) the nature and purpose of the agreement; (iii) the degree of market power of the merged firm; (iv) entry barriers; and (v) the trend toward concentration in the industry. More controversial, however, is the fact that the decision found that the merger should be deemed illegal, pursuant to § 7 of the Clayton Act, even though it would likely lead to lower prices for consumers:

> Not only may this merger, judged from a vertical standpoint, affect manufacturers who compete with Brown; it may also adversely affect competition on the retailing level. With a large manufacturer such as Brown behind it, the Kinney chain would have a great competitive advantage over the retail stores with which it vies for consumer patronage. As a manufacturer-owned outlet, the Kinney store would doubtless be able to sell its shoes at a lower profit margin and outlast an independent competitor. The merger would also effectively prevent the retail competitor from dealing in Brown shoes, since these might be offered at lower prices in Kinney stores than elsewhere.

In Pabst Brewing (1966), the Supreme Court found that the merger between Pabst Brewing Company and Blatz Brewing Company violated § 7 of the Clayton Act even though it resulted only in a 4%-combined market share in national market for beer sales. Opposing the decision of the District Court for the Eastern District of Wisconsin, the Supreme Court concluded that "proof of the section of the country where the anticompetitive effect exists" was not required, but only "subsidiary to the crucial § 7 question, which is whether the merger may substantially lessen competition anywhere in the country." Similarly, in Von's Grocery (1966), the Supreme Court reversed the decision of the lower court and ordered the divestiture of the deal concerning a merger where the merged entity would have a 7.5%-combined market share.

But more particularly, populist antitrust materializes in three distinctive ways. First, antitrust populists see monopolies and abusive practices everywhere, despite well-accepted economic analysis. In an articulately titled book Monopoly Sucks, Sally Hubbard claims the "Monopolies pervade our everyday lives in ways we don't realize [...] But America's monopoly crisis is not just about Big Tech. It's big health care, big agriculture, Big Pharma, big...pick an industry, any industry. Big everything. Our economy is ruled by behemoths because decades ago, our government chose to dismantle anti-monopoly laws and policies."[22] Just to clarify that the term "monopoly" is given no specific meaning by antitrust populists, Hubbard feels the need to specify that "To keep things simple, throughout the book when I refer to 'monopolies,' I'm using it as shorthand for monopolies, duopolies, and oligopolies."[23] To define monopoly by one thing and its contrary does not seem to overburden antitrust populists. Indeed, using an extremely narrow definition of relevant markets for antitrust purposes,[24] antitrust populists consider a company with a mere market power as "monopoly."

Antitrust populists see monopolies everywhere, and most notoriously, confuse modern large corporations with the English Crown monopolies against which the American founders vilipended.[25] Whereas these Crown monopolies were legally created and protected monopolies with special privileges and some advantages (some predated are patent and copyright laws), antitrust populists consciously confuse legal monopolies with factually, meritoriously created large corporations. The former is insulated from competition and derives from political discretion. The latter emerges out of competition and innovation and derives from consumer sovereignty. Thus, to consider that the Tea Party rebellion was a fight against monopolies while overlooking that these corporations were State created is erroneous and insincere.[26]

Consequently, to unearth Jefferson's writings against Crown monopolies to argue that American founders would not let today's large corporations exist is historically wrong and conceptually deceiving.[27] Moreover, antitrust populists' use of a misconceived "Jeffersonian democracy" is

[22] Hubbard (2020:3–4).

[23] Hubbard (2020:14).

[24] Portuese (2022).

[25] Raj (2017).

[26] Lynn (2010, 2020); Klobuchar (2021:21–30).

[27] Mossoff (2007).

imprudent: Not only Jefferson merely despised legally created monopolistic rights for special economic privileges, but even for the area of invention and innovation, Jefferson advocated for inventors to enjoy legal protection.[28]

Because of the combined effect of the narrow definition of relevant markets and the lack of coherent meaning ascribed to "monopoly," antitrust populists consider that monopolies are everywhere, as illustrated in the House Report on Big Tech.[29] Nadler & Cicilline state that "Facebook has monopoly power in the market for the social network"[30]; "Apple exerts monopoly power in the mobile app store market, controlling access to more than 100 million iPhones and iPads in the U.S."[31]; Google "now enjoys durable monopoly power in the market for the general online search"[32]; Amazon "has monopoly power over most third-party sellers and many of its suppliers."[33] Any large company with a sizeable market share, albeit in a non-dominant market position, may seldom be qualified as a "monopoly" by antitrust populists.

Second, after having confused large companies with monopolies, antitrust populists ascribe to antitrust laws a role of fighting bigness for the benefit of smallness. Antitrust populists may try to convince that "antimonopoly does not mean 'big is bad.'[34] The New Brandeisians– like Justice Brandeis–recognize that certain industries tend naturally towards monopoly."[35] And yet, because "monopolies" mean mere large corporations, Brandeisians believe that "big is bad." Indeed, large corporations have become large essentially because of superior efficiency, unmatched innovations, or "business acumen."[36] However,

[28] Matsuura (2008).

[29] Nadler & Cicilline (2020).

[30] Nadler & Cicilline (2020:12).

[31] Nadler & Cicilline (2020:16).

[32] Nadler & Cicilline (2020:177).

[33] Nadler & Cicilline (2020:257).

[34] Kessler (2021).

[35] Khan (2018:131).

[36] United States v. Grinnell Corp. 384 U.S. 563, 57,071 (1966).

antitrust populists perceive these business advantages as "unfair advantages." In Brandeisian rhetoric, antitrust populists argue that large corporations are somehow "cursed" since the size problem materializes with "dis-economies" of scale.

To illustrate his point, Wu refers to the business of making pizza: "Making pizza efficiently requires little more than an industrial oven [...] The advantages, if any, are those related to size, power, reputation, and so on–compare the Domino's chain to the local pizzeria–but are not related to the ability to make a better product."[37] To demonstrate how diseconomies of scale may justify that bigger is not always better in the tech sector by using the example of a homogenous and easily comparable good such as pizza amounts to an economic mistake and an anecdotal error. Antitrust populists disseminate "some versions of the popular view that reflexively conclude that 'big is bad.' This view sees the rise of large corporations [...] as the proper focus of antitrust enforcement. The big-is-bad view aims, as I see it, at the wrong target for antitrust enforcers."[38] The superior efficiency of large corporations no longer, for antitrust populists, demonstrates efficiencies but rather represents evidence of unfair competitive advantage.

Because the 'antitrust populism' here defined abandons the consumer welfare standard, hence any account for efficiency, the lower efficiency of smaller competitors does not prevent the competitive process from protecting these competitors from larger rivals artificially.[39] Ignoring larger corporations' considerable economic and social benefits, antitrust populists find an inherent virtue in securing small business units even if this amounts to higher prices and lower innovation for final consumers, even if they do so without expressly confessing it.[40] What Neo-Brandeisians claim is that the consumer welfare standard is not enough for capturing all of the anticompetitive practices, nor to address the competition concerns arising from mergers, in today's economy.

Third, antitrust populists prefer the radical, liberty-intrusive, and property rights-negating remedy of structural remedies in their anti-bigness rhetoric: Antitrust populists want to break up large companies, leaving

[37] Wu (2018:69).

[38] Hesse (2016).

[39] Crane (2018).

[40] Hovenkamp (2019).

open question the "optimal" size and the question of the expected tangible benefits in the long run. Populist antitrust not only derails the consumer welfare standard and the economic analysis of antitrust laws, but it also blurs the analysis in favor of a deconcentration objective at the expense of associated benefits of corporate consolidations. To justify companies' break-ups, antitrust populists claim that the market has excessively concentrated.[41]

However, data reveals that several industries in the US economy became less concentrated from 2002 to 2017.[42] Moreover, the US antitrust agencies themselves contest the very claim that markets have concentrated to a significant extent: "The U.S. Department of Justice (Department) and Federal Trade Commission (collectively, the U.S. Agencies) find the claims of increasing concentration are unsupported by data for meaningful markets."[43] Thus, the economy's claims are mainly unfounded as they frequently appear throughout economic history.[44]

However, the rationale for breaking up companies lies in the assumption that there is excessive concentration. And yet, Wu claims that "since the year 2000, across US industries the measures of market concentration have increased in over 75 per cent of industries."[45] In support of his claim, Wu cites Grullon et al., who nevertheless qualify their findings' implications by noting that "although a greater concentration of product markets can improve the quality, or increase the variety, of products offered, whether those changes are sufficient to compensate customers for firms' higher profit margins remains an open question [...] Future research should focus on the welfare implications of our empirical findings."[46] Consequently, increased concentration has mixed welfare implications contrary to Brandeisians, who equate corporation concentration with economic welfare harm. Increased concentration leads to increased productivity and increased output, but no price changes.[47]

[41] Abdela & Steinbaum (2018).

[42] Atkinson & Lage de Sousa (2021).

[43] United States (2018:2).

[44] Kennedy (2020).

[45] Wu (2020:12).

[46] Grullon et al. (2019:735).

[47] Ganapati (2020).

Thus, increased concentration has not produced increased profitability in manufacturing.[48]

Therefore, increased concentration may result from increased efficiency and innovation, not in monopolistic rents—in line with Schumpeterian and Chandler's analysis.[49] Even assuming that markets have concentrated, this does not mean that antitrust laws have failed.[50] Antitrust populists consider that, despite the lack of increased market concentration substantially, companies need to be broken up to address the alleged "monopoly problem."[51] Antitrust structural remedies are antitrust populists' most favored solutions to a misidentified problem.

In addition to fighting market concentration through ex-post intervention, Brandeisians advocate that deconcentration should be pursued by means of stricter and more comprehensive ex-ante regulation. If populist antitrust is the general anti-bigness tendency of Brandeisians, precautionary antitrust is the Brandeisians' specific tendency to favor regulation over antitrust enforcement.

2 Precautionary Antitrust

Abstract

Brandeis advocated for regulated competition to prevent private monopolies and implemented the FTC Act of 1914. Neo-Brandeisians now advocate for regulation over antitrust enforcement, favoring a precautionary approach. This approach, rooted in European values and Ordoliberalism, aims to safeguard competition and democratic values. Other jurisdictions are exploring precautionary antitrust measures for digital markets as well. However, the shift toward regulation raises concerns about the role of courts and the potential for over-regulation. Brandeisians can inform modern antitrust measures, but a cautious approach is necessary to ensure a fair and competitive market environment.

Brandeis favored regulation over antitrust. In 1912, he explained why he favored the "regulation of competition" over the "regulation of

48 Shapiro (2017).

49 Schumpeter (1942); Chandler (1990).

50 United States (2018:5–6).

51 Teachout (2020); Wu (2018); Hawley (2021a, 2021b).

monopoly": He ridiculed Teddy Roosevelt's new party (the Progressive Party) to "legalize monopoly" because it is inevitable, and advocated that "private monopoly in the industry is never permissible; it is never desirable and is not inevitable."[52] When Brandeis referred to "monopoly," he, of course, used its populist (not economic) meaning and thereby merely meant large businesses. Indeed, he theorized the concept of "regulated competition."[53] Brandeis considered that "competition can be reserved, and where it is suppressed, can be restored."[54] Because competition meant rivalry among small businesses absent large companies, Brandeis advocated for ex-ante rules that would prevent the emergence of "private monopolies"—i.e., large firms. In other words, Brandeis was not a trust-buster. He aimed to be a trust-avoider: Regulated competition rather than regulated monopolies should ensure a limited version of the competition. Brandeis believed in limiting competition to preserve it: Big businesses had to see their rights limited.

In contrast, small businesses had to see their right to "industrial liberty" legally protected. This Brandeisian approach led to promote ex-ante competition rules rather than ex-post antitrust enforcement in courts. This very Brandeisian approach permeates in today's calls and reforms for moving away from both antitrust and courts in favor of ex-ante regulatory compliance rules on competition. Brandeis implemented the idea of regulated competition essentially with the passage of the FTC Act of 1914: The competition process would become ongoing monitoring of companies' sizes via regulatory compliance rather than by a mere judicial process of antitrust lawsuits. Similarly, the Clayton Act of 1914 instituted a system of ex-ante merger control, replacing the idea of ex-post trust-busting of mergers and combinations.

Now, Neo-Brandeisians also want to rely on regulation rather than antitrust enforcement. Aiming at taking antitrust "away from the courts," antitrust populists disparage the role of the courts, vilipend the elaboration of the antitrust case law, and require "timely" interventions in the market to rein in large corporations. Timely here means preventative interventions. More precisely, it means a precautionary logic toward market competition and innovative conduct. Before the harm may even

[52] Brandeis (1912).

[53] Berk (2009).

[54] Brandeis (1912).

materialize, competition regulation may preclude given conduct from being allowed, often at the expense of the pro-competitive and pro-innovative effects of such conduct. The view of regulating anticompetitive conduct no longer via antitrust enforcement but rather by ex-ante regulation follows a precautionary logic. Indeed, the fundamental elements of the precautionary principles are increasingly present for justifying the regulation of competition with ex-ante rules.[55]

The precautionary approach to antitrust disparages the role of courts, laments against the time-consuming and uncertainties inherent to the judicial process, favors interventions based on risks rather than demonstrated harms, shifts the burden of proof so that companies are liable unless proven otherwise, and believes in the irreversibility of market positions over the continuous process of creative destruction. Timely, urgent, preventative—in short, ex-ante—interventions trump ex-post enforcement. As these interventions target rapidly changing markets with innovative companies, precautionary antitrust often clashes with innovation-based antitrust. Regardless, precautionary antitrust represents the alleged benefit of ensuring the protection of innovation laggards and smaller firms.

Precautionary antitrust has emerged in Europe with Ordoliberalism; precautionary antitrust now enters America via the Neo-Brandeisians.[56] Ordoliberalism emerged in Europe in the late 20s, notably in Germany, in response to the crisis of the Weimar Republic. The theory was developed by economists and legal scholars of the Freiburg School, including Walter Eucken and Franz Böhm.[57] According to the Ordoliberals, such economic downfall had been caused by the corporativism predominant in the country back then, which resulted in the capture of the state by economic interests.[58] Ordoliberalism understood that the Weimar welfare state facilitated private organization's interests to thrive, considering that unions and employer federations were given a great amount of power. "Unions, capitalist interest organizations, corporatism, codetermination and collective wage bargaining were therefore regarded with suspicion by

[55] Portuese (2020, 2021c).

[56] Portuese (2020b).

[57] Felice & Vatiero (2014).

[58] Hien (2023).

the ordoliberals."[59] This emerging school of thinking claimed a strong state intervention to counterbalance private power, advocating in favor of a hard currency, a fierce competition policy, and a rejection of the welfare state.

Ordoliberalism is considered by scholars as having played great influence in the shaping of European law, notably competition law.[60] According to the Ordoliberals, antitrust policy was an important tool to control both the economic and political powers of big companies. By increasing its role in the economy, firms could translate its economic strength into political power, harming not only a country's free market, but also putting democracy at stake. Hence, under the ordoliberal perspective, states had to adopt active measures to inhibit companies from restraining competition (e.g., through collusion) and to safeguard democratic values, including individual liberties.

Having said that, on the one hand, Ordoliberals rely considerably on a precautionary approach, whereby state should intervene in the economy by adopting widespread laws and a strong institutional framework (the "Ordo"). On the other hand, the fight against cartels that existed in the Weimar Republic was a central goal of Ordoliberalism, showing that this line of thinking also has a repressive, ex-post nature.

Unsurprisingly, Brandeisians see in the European precautionary approach to competition a basis for inspiration. Indeed, European competition increasingly inspires Brandeisians. For instance, Wu refers to the "Chicago virus,"[61] which has "infected" Europe's Ordoliberal view of competition that allegedly best preserves competition. He considers that "Europe deserves credit for the fact that it now leads in the scrutiny of 'big tech'."[62] Also, in June 2021, New York altered its antitrust laws to integrate the European concept of abuse of dominant position—a much stringent concept compared to "monopolization" of Sect. 2of the Sherman Act.[63] Also, in June 2021, Rep. David Cicilline (D-RI)

[59] Hien (2023).

[60] Felice & Vatiero (2014).

[61] Wu (2020:79).

[62] Wu (2020:103).

[63] Tracy (2021).

presented five bills to Congress which directly borrow from the European Digital Markets Act's precautionary logic of regulating competition.[64]

Recently, the European Commission's Digital Markets Act ("DMA") represents the pinnacle of European precautionary antitrust.[65] Although it contains some exceptional provisions, its nature is mainly of an ex-ante regulation. The proactive designation of "gatekeepers" shifts the burden of proof on companies, whose practices are deemed presumably anticompetitive until proven otherwise. Absent evidence of harm, the mere hypothetical risk that conduct may ultimately harm "the structure of the market" or represent "structural risks to competition," with a threat of irreversibly altering the market, such a risk suffices to justify a precautionary prohibition. Explicitly borrowing the precautionary rhetoric to digital competition, the Digital Markets Act illustrates the powerful deterrent effect of regulation on innovation incentives for the sake of preservation of the status quo, the preservation of the current competitors, and the associated market structure.

Other jurisdictions are trying to implement precautionary antitrust in order to regulate ex-ante digital markets, including Australia, Germany, France, Italy, Japan, Brazil,[66] and the United Kingdom.[67] In fact similarly to the DMA, some of these acts of regulation propose to identify and tackle the power of big companies. For instance, the draft of the Digital Markets, Competition, and Consumers Bill in the United Kingdom proposes specific obligations for firms that have "Strategic Market Status" (SMS), despite recognizing the importance of enabling innovation to thrive:

> While recognising the many benefits digital markets bring to people and businesses, the Government has set out that the new pro-competition regime should address the far-reaching market power of a small number of technology firms by enabling the CMA [Competition and Markets Authority] to proactively drive more dynamic digital markets and prevent harmful practices that hold back innovation and growth. It has recognised that there are specific features of fast-moving digital markets that can lead

[64] Kang (2021).

[65] Portuese (2021b).

[66] Parisi (2024).

[67] OECD (2021).

> to a small number of firms establishing entrenched and substantial market power, which the existing competition framework is not set up to address.

In the United States, recent attempts to impose additional regulation have been undertaken, including the "American Choice and Innovation Online Act," "Ending Platform Monopolies Act," "Platform Competition and Opportunity Act of 2021," "Merger Filing Fee Modernization Act of 2021," and the "Augmenting Compatibility and Competition by Enabling Service Switching Act of 2021" bills.

More specifically, Brandeisians advocate for ex-ante rules via the FTC's rulemaking power. For example, the Open Market Institute, the American Economic Liberties Project, and many other policy initiatives representing the Neo-Brandeisian approach to antirust have petitioned for Rulemaking to Prohibit Exclusionary Contracts.[68] After petitioning for the prohibition of non-compete clauses,[69] the petition on the prohibition of exclusionary contracts reveals the Brandeisians' willingness to enforce a per se illegality (or precautionary prohibition) to contracts that may or may not yield pro-competitive and pro-innovative consequences depending on each case's circumstances. Willing to extrapolate the Magnuson-Moss Warranty Act of 1975, which empowered the FTC to improve consumer protection, Brandeisians call for rulemaking in the area of regulating ex-ante competition with prohibitions on contracts with exclusivity requirements.[70] Indeed, they believe that antitrust should further prohibit conduct in their incipiency, as suggested by the FTC and Clayton Acts of 1914, for which Brandeis was instrumental:

> Like the other landmark antitrust statute of 1914 (the Clayton Act), the FTC Act is an incipiency statute and accordingly prohibits unfair competitive practices well before they actually restrain trade or create, maintain, or extend a monopoly. Consequently, the FTC can identify and prohibit unfair competitive practices before they rise to the level of illegal monopolization under the Sherman Act. The Supreme Court has applied this legislative purpose in its interpretation of the FTC Act. Accordingly, practices like exclusive dealing and tying can violate the FTC Act without necessarily

[68] Open Markets Institute et al. (2020).

[69] Open Markets Institute et al. (2019).

[70] Open Markets Institute (2020:4).

> violating the Sherman Act. A reasonable possibility of unfairly excluding rivals or injuring consumers is enough.

Brandeisians advocate for greater rulemaking power to undermine the rule of reason approach antitrust cases (whereby each case weighs out pro-competitive and anticompetitive effects of given conduct). This is made clear as part of a broader critique against the role of the courts in antitrust: Risk-averse administrative rules should arguably substitute a fact-based judicial process (Open Markets Institute 2020:74). These petitions led Acting Chairwoman Rebecca Kelly Slaughter to demonstrate increased interest in rulemaking.[71] Brandeisians' leading voice and FTC Commissioner, Lina Khan, made the argument explicit when she advocated for rulemaking in regulated competition:

> First, rulemaking would enable the Commission to issue clear rules to give market participants sufficient notice about what the laws, helping ensure that enforcement is predictable [...] Second, establishing rules could help relieve antitrust enforcement of steep costs and prolonged trials.[72]

The first argument of greater legal certainty is a legitimate one, but the second argument of avoiding the judiciary is unsustainable: Any (antitrust) case takes time and generates litigation costs. If this argument is further developed, virtually any antitrust case appears unreasonably time-consuming and inadequately costly. This misguided logic can further be extended to any area of law so that administrative rules should take precedence over judicial review. As a result, access to justice and the right of defense as fundamental rights become under threat. Moreover, the idea that the FTC should define unfair methods of competition contradicts the 1920 Supreme Court case of Gratz.[73]

And yet, Brandeisians primarily advocate for taking antitrust away from the courts so that risk-averse enforcers can enforce antitrust principles at their incipiency according to the fundamental elements of the precautionary principle—namely, a shift of the burden of proof, intervention in the absence of harm, preference for preserving the status quo over disruption and innovation. Indeed, Chopra & Khan frame the "choice

[71] Slaughter (2021).

[72] Chopra & Khan (2020:367–368).

[73] FTC v. Gratz, 253 U.S. 421 (1920).

between adjudication and participatory rulemaking,"[74] thereby wrongly suggesting that adjudication is not participatory. It is also wrong to suggest that rulemaking involves participatory dialogue. In contrast, firms have to comply with rules without possibilities to counter-argue efficiencies since rulemaking's raison d'être is the opposite of the rule of reason. Moreover, having to comply with several, different rules from different jurisdictions increases companies' costs of doing business.[75] By facing higher struggles, companies might eventually have to pass-it-on to consumers, either by increasing prices or reducing, and even ceasing the offering of certain products and services.

More dramatically, Sitaraman attacks the role of the courts in antitrust cases and advocates for administratively enforced antitrust rules:

> [A] timid FTC has failed to take up its congressionally-authorized role and has largely abandoned the project of making regulations to interpret and enforce the antitrust laws it administers. This has left the Supreme Court to define the substance of antitrust law. This is a serious problem. Agencies have considerable expertise and are politically accountable to Congress and the President. In contrast, the Court is made up of unelected, unaccountable judges who have no expertise in business realities or any specific sector of the economy.[76]

This argument of courts being un-knowledgeable about economic issues can be made for any cases involving economic matters (virtually every case), thereby suggesting undermining the judiciary's power. Although a crucial pillar to democracy, the judiciary would then be deprived of reviewing economic liberties, economic rights such as property rights, freedom of contract, and freedom to conduct business on the mere basis that these cases are too complex for the judge to apprehend. Brandeisian antitrust certainly push for an idea of regulated competition. But "how much Brandeis do the Neo-Brandeisians want,"[77] given the real risks such ideology causes to democratic principles? Over-regulation of competition certainly would lead to the creeping precautionary logic entering US antitrust doctrines via risk-averse and "timely" interventions.

[74] Chopra & Khan (2020).

[75] Bradford (2023).

[76] Sitaraman (2018:8).

[77] Crane (2019).

This is similar to the precautionary principle that has already come to the fore in European antitrust.[78] The concerns about courts acting on antitrust issues are not news, Borkian antitrust has also endorsed it.[79] But, differently, Neo-Brandeisians go a step beyond and use such criticism to advocate for more ex-ante regulation.

3 Popular Antitrust

Abstract

Brandeisian antitrust advocates for popular antitrust, focusing on competition, inequality, and democracy. It opposes technocratic analysis by experts and advocates for a more accessible approach to enforcement. Critics of monopolies overlook the potential benefits of capitalism. Neo-Brandeisianism advocates specifically for a return to antitrust enforcement without considering economic analysis. Ordoliberalism shares similarities with Brandeisian values, emphasizing fairness and market competition. This subchapter argues that the balance between efficiency and societal welfare should be prioritized in shaping antitrust policy for the future.

The third and final trait of Brandeisian antitrust, beyond being economically deconcentrationist with antitrust populism and being technically deterrent to innovation with precautionary antitrust, is that Brandeisian antitrust flourish as part of popular antitrust – namely, a vision of competition aligned with the one allegedly desired by the people, and in conflict with the vision of experts. Despite this fact, the Sherman Act of 1890 embraced a common law model whereby antitrust laws would develop "outside the sphere of politics."[80] Thus, Brandeisians fight against a technocratic antitrust, where the economic analysis of antitrust laws prevails in favor of a more popular antitrust.

Indeed, antitrust, especially the economic analysis of antitrust laws, predominantly remained "technocratic" given the efficiencies arguments and complex discussions often involved in enforcing these cases.[81] Indeed, Hovenkamp considers that "over the last fifty years antitrust has

[78] Portuese (2020b, 2021b, 2021c).

[79] Jacobs (1995:219); Hovenkamp (2005:76).

[80] Voorhees (2014).

[81] Elhauge (2018).

become much more technical, particularly in areas such as merger enforcement and exclusionary behavior, but also in more collateral areas such as assessing causation and measuring damages."[82] Technocratic antitrust law and economics presumably over-complexify antitrust enforcement by failing to make "nontechnocratic arguments that are understandable to the general public."[83] Technical discussions by experts allegedly contradict the purpose of antitrust law.[84] Some Neo-Brandeisians express the concern that "antitrust focus' has become exclusively and narrowly economic" and "the very ideal of political role has all but disappeared."[85]

To demonize "monopolies" (which merely are large businesses), Brandeis argued that only the prohibition of big business could preserve competition—the mere prohibition of anticompetitive conduct does not suffice. To make his argument compelling to the public audience, he dramatizes the effect of allowing large firms to survive: These firms would be tyrants living above the law while the American people would abide by the law:

> Now, gentlemen, see what [legalizing monopoly] implies. It implies that there are at least some fields of industry in which we are to accept private monopoly, and it indicates something which, to my mind, is far more important even than being divided on the great question whether we shall have monopoly or competition. [...] Realize, gentlemen, what this means. It means that we must state solemnly that the power of the American people to enforce law is not absolute; that there are a few individuals who stand superior to the American people.[86]

These exaggerated claims—namely, large companies cannot be subject to the law—ideally, fuel the populist rhetoric of Brandeis. But, more specifically, it aims at moving away from an economic analysis of antitrust enforcement mainly focused on the consumer welfare standard in favor of a more popular approach to competition, that contemplate other standards as well, including addressing inequality and protecting democracy.[87]

[82] Hovenkamp (2018:585).

[83] Elhauge (2018).

[84] Wu (2018:128).

[85] Wu (2018:54).

[86] Brandeis (1912).

[87] Wu (2018:23).

After all, the "People's lawyer" legitimately advocates for a people's approach:

> [T]here is no longer in America equality before the law; that the rich man has such control over affairs in America that the poor and less able worker cannot secure his rights according to the American Constitution, and they have, therefore, resorted to violence.[88]

Because Brandeisians antitrust is popular antitrust, it inherently carries an anti-expert stance. Judges and academics are ideal targets for Brandeis antitrust because they arguably preserve the interests of the economic establishments. Still, economists and experts prove to be Brandeisians' bête noire as they advance an agenda that allegedly thwarts the general public interest. Brandeis opposed this view of technical antitrust made by economic and legal experts: He favored the perspective of the "people" to emphasize the "despotism" of the trusts and other oligarchs which imperil "our institutions."[89] Brandeis, despite later being a Supreme Court Justice, portrayed himself as no expert—he preferred being an advocate, a political figure:

> Although Brandeis was not an academic thinker [...], he rarely lost an opportunity to articulate the broader implications of practical problems. And when he did, he sounded much like the republican antimonopoly movements that went before him: the self-styled 'producers' of the Greenback-Labor Party, the Knights of Labor, and the Farmer's Alliance. Like them, Brandeis' first questions about the economy were moral and political, not technical.[90]

Brandeis' populist lineage chastised experts' advice in favor of a populist rhetoric of a powerful oligarchy striping the American people and behaving above the law. This rhetoric is well-shared by Neo-Brandeisians, who also advocate for a popular antitrust instead of technical/technocratic antitrust. Indeed, Brandeisians Khan & Teachout write that "oligarchy or monopolization in one realm (political or economic) leads to monopolization and oligarchy in the other. Unfortunately, this belief has fallen into

[88] Brandeis (1912).

[89] Berk (2009:45).

[90] Berk (2009:42).

desuetude in law as legal scholarship has built up a division between the study of economic and political power."[91] Allegedly, "an economic dictatorship would lead to political dictatorship."[92] This belief has legitimately fallen into desuetude until the Brandeisians' revival because it is erroneous: Big business does not prevent democratic principles from being held firmly in republican institutions. One example is the New Deal and World War II eras during which Franklin D. Roosevelt had a more lenient policy toward large corporations at a time when the democratic principles of the United States have never been so firmly held, both domestically and internationally.

This unfounded belief that concentrated economic power leads to political despotism, the end of democracy, and other catastrophic consequences wrongly infer from the Nazis' use of German cartels to implement their plans—overlooking the fact that neither Mussolini's Italy, Vichy's France, or Japan needed to have cartels similar to the Germans to turn their democratic principles wary. Moreover, powerful capitalist corporations often are barriers to fascism rather than paths to it. England's and America's adherence to capitalist principles of free competition and strongly enforcer property rights may explain the lack of progress of fascist ideas in these countries. And yet, Brandeisians regularly resort to this flawed argument that concentrated economic power would lead to fascism and despotism. Indeed, they support the populists' claim that the Sherman Act was passed because they believed that "concentration of economic power concentrates political power, posing a threat to democracy akin to monarchy or dictatorship."[93] Aside from the confusion between monarchies and democracies (indeed, many monarchies are democracies), the idea that large corporations lead to dictatorship remains deceptive. Yet, Brandeisians extensively use it to call for a more popular antitrust.[94]

As an illustration, Barry Lynn, the Brandeisian advocating for populist antitrust, once authored an article with Phillip Longman titled "Populism with a Brain" where he justifies the idea of aggressive antimonopoly

[91] Khan & Teachout (2014:37).

[92] Wu (2019:1′28).

[93] Khan & Vaheesan (2017:265).

[94] Foge (2019).

enforcement based on the need to have a populist stance against "oligarchs":

> The Populists would certainly have supported Sanders's call for public financing of campaigns and his embrace of "Break Up the Banks." But the men and women who rose against America's oligarchs of a century ago would have been deeply dismayed that no candidate in 2016 has taken a strong stand against monopoly [...] What would a True Populist do today? Immediately restore America's traditional anti-monopoly philosophy, most importantly in the guidelines that determine how enforcers view the purpose of these laws, and start breaking up today's monopolies.[95]

The Brandeisian's idea to deconcentrate economic power and to disparage "technical battles of experts"[96] lead to a risk that antitrust "may be taken away from experts or that experts will yield to the pressure."[97] The populist skepticism against experts inherent to Brandeisian antitrust leads advocates calling for a more significant role for the Congress and administrative agencies where a so-called "participatory" dialogue with the people may allegedly occur.[98] The skepticism toward experts, especially economic experts, is not only a criticism of antitrust law & economics in general, but it is also a pledge for substituting a "public interest standard" to the consumer welfare standard: The citizens, and not consumers, will be the primary concern under Brandeisian antitrust. This open-textured objective runs the risk of greater arbitrariness in antitrust enforcement.[99] Nevertheless, the citizens' perspective of popular antitrust, as opposed to the consumer's perspective of technocratic antitrust, is grounded on the premise that "We, the People" can similarly fight private concentrated power the Constitution held the fight against concentrated political power.

Senator Klobuchar (D-MN)'s book Antitrust—Taking on Monopoly Power From the Gilded Age to the Digital Age clarifies that Brandeisian antitrust is a popular version of antitrust where the people can effectively

[95] Lynn & Longman (2016).

[96] Wu (2018:128).

[97] Lamadrid de Pablo (2017:147).

[98] Chopra & Khan (2020).

[99] Portuese (2022).

oppose the experts.[100] Indeed, in her staunch advocacy for Brandeisian antitrust for twenty-first-century America, Senator Klobuchar confuses large private companies with State-created monopolies of the English Crown to try to explain that the very founding of America was the people's fight against large companies purportedly referred erroneously as "monopolies":

> Thus, or country's Declaration of Independence from England was not only a political Declaration of Independence from a foreign country but also an act of economic rebellion against monopoly power. Back then, the colonies who even tried to compete against the British monopoly mercenaries could be fined or improved by the Crown's prosecutors [...] One memorable example back in the 1770s of British efforts to impose a monopoly on American's colonists? Tea. [...] The colonists were protesting the English Parliament's Teac Act because they believed it violated their rights to 'no taxation without representation'.[101]

Senator Klobuchar brings the rhetoric of the people suppressed by monopolies further when she writes:

> Thriving competitive companies are essential to our economy and to our American way of life, but we must never forget who built America –its workers –and who the U.S. Constitution puts in charge of the government: "We the People," not "We the Corporations," or "We the Monopolies." When America's founders set up our country, they railed against the power of the British East India Company and worried about other abuses of power. But truth be told, they could never have conceived of the sheer size of modern, multinational companies or of the enormous influence they now have.[102]

To be sure, America's founders could never have conceived smartphones and augmented reality, nor would they have conceived the enormous influence and information each citizen has thanks to Internet access. In other words, taking the citizen's perspective to address an economic question necessarily leads to populist answers out of touch with today's real concerns. Nevertheless, Senator Klobuchar calls for a

[100] Klobuchar (2021).

[101] Klobuchar (2021:21).

[102] Klobuchar (2021:177).

popular antitrust to emerge although she is a member of the political establishment:

> It is time for Americans – for "We the People" – to reclaim our power. What the United States needs now is a renewed antitrust movement – one that is grounded in competitive economic policies and sets forth a pro-competition agenda.[103]

The last line of the 600-page book reveals the anti-expert stance inherent to Brandeis antitrust as where writes:

> It is now crystal clear that the antitrust laws must be seriously updated and made relevant again as part of a reinvigorated American competition policy. [...] Everyone in America deserves a fair shot –and an honest opportunity –when it comes to realizing the American Dream. But enough words have been written. And enough experts have weighed in.[104]

Popular antitrust is one of the facets of Brandeisian antitrust. We identified the two other facets—populist and precautionary antitrust—that prove to also depart dramatically from antitrust law & economics. To revive an economic analysis of antitrust laws without necessarily reverting to the Chicago School's model of perfect competition. The Chicago School evolved to become closer to its main rival—the structuralist Harvard School—to form a broad consensus. Indeed, Richard Posner once wrote, "changes in mind within both the Chicago school and its principal rival, which I have called the Harvard school, have produced a steady trend toward convergence. Differences remain, but increasingly they are technical rather than ideological."[105]

However, Neo-Brandeisianism perturbs such consensus for a return to antitrust enforcement before the law & economics movement, thereby overlooking the economic knowledge amassed during these years and the jurisprudential evolution elaborated throughout decades. In the next part, we argue that it is possible to move away from this consensus without embracing Brandeisian antitrust and ignoring an economic analysis of antitrust laws. Indeed, a new antitrust law & economics approach is

[103] Klobuchar (2021:351).

[104] Klobuchar (2021:355).

[105] Posner (1979:948).

needed. Otherwise, a politically driven and technically inconclusive Brandeisian antitrust would last more than a generation. Such a new antitrust law & economics approach can develop based on evolutionary economics and a dynamic approach to competition. The economist Joseph Schumpeter pioneered such an approach. It is now time to embrace, operationalize, and implement it. We now consider such an enthusiastic future for antitrust policy.

Ordoliberalism resembles Brandeisian values. Both believe that antitrust policy should create a "level playing field and economic opportunity".[106] Under the Ordoliberalism perspective, antitrust policy is intertwined with other values that are not entirely economic, considering that the goals of the state intervention should be fighting excessive private's both economic and political power, in order to preserve democracy. Both Ordoliberals and Neo-Brandeisians beliefs align closely with respect that markets should respect a strong social, political, and moral framework.[107] Neo-Brandeisians, by reawakening Justice Brandeis' values, advocate that non-purely market driven values should be addressed by competition policy, including helping small and medium-sized companies, tackling social inequality and protecting democracy.[108]

This broadening of the scope of antitrust policy, which is a common approach of the Ordoliberalism, Brandeisian and Neo-Brandeisian movements, risk placing efficiency and, more notably, innovation, in a marginal role within the scrutiny of antitrust agencies.

Having discussed the main tenets of Brandeisian antitrust, one should bear in mind that, being a public policy undertaken by governments, antitrust is subject to values, and it is up to governments to decide on which values they will rely antitrust policy.[109] In this sense, antitrust will never be apolitical.[110] Values, however, divert in their nature: While some advocate for economic, efficient values, others argue antitrust should

[106] Crane (2020:1331).

[107] Wu (2018:82).

[108] Fox (2022).

[109] Allensworth (2016).

[110] Crane (2007).

pursue non-economic goals.[111] In this book, we demonstrate that efficiency, and, more importantly, dynamic efficiency, should be the value to be prioritized.

[111] Ayal (2014); Ezrachi (2017).

CHAPTER 3

Schumpeterian Antitrust Under Rise

Abstract The Schumpeterian competition theory suggests that innovation drives competition. This particular theory is gaining traction in antitrust debates, as the model emphasizes workable competition, promoting innovation and dynamic competition. Furthermore, it suggests that antitrust agencies should reform their laws to accommodate changing economic landscapes, incorporating Schumpeterian competition and recognizing the nuanced relationship between market power, innovation, and competition. Critics of this school of thought argue that traditional models of static price competition do not effectively address the complexities of innovation in today's markets. The chapter provides a comprehensive overview of the Schumpeterian competition theory, and expands upon The Antitrust Modernization Committee's views, which recognize the importance of innovation in rethinking antitrust enforcement, but suggest adjustments to align antitrust policy with dynamic efficiency theories and prioritize Schumpeterian competition in competitive assessments.

Keywords Antitrust agencies · Neo-Brandeisians · Innovation · Market · Schumpeterian · Herbert Hovenkamp · Enforcement

A. Portuese, *The Battle for the Future of Antitrust*, Palgrave Studies in Institutions, Economics and Law, https://doi.org/10.1007/978-3-031-75794-5_3

The way antitrust enforcers have traditionally assessed the level of competition in a market remained through the lens of the idealized model of perfect competition. According to that viewpoint, the role of antitrust agencies is to restore, and alternative to tending to, the state of perfect competition. This idealized model of perfect competition describes a market whereby no firms would enjoy market power because the competitive constraints would be so intense that firms could only set their prices to the "competitive optimum"—meaning at the marginal cost of producing one additional output.

This model of perfect competition is both unrealistic and undesirable. Economists such as John Maurice Clark explained that perfect competition is unrealistic and, most importantly, economically undesirable. But no better economist than Joseph Schumpeter has vilipended the model of perfect competition and suggested an alternative model: The model of imperfect competition whereby firms with market power are in a state of disequilibrium and are bound to innovate to compete effectively. Schumpeterian theorized a model of competition—later referred to as "Schumpeterian Competition"—which categorically diverges from the model of perfect competition.

According to Schumpeterian competition, innovation is not simply a by-product of competition: It is the source of competition.[1] In other words, Schumpeterian competition does not necessarily perceive competition as the cause of innovation but rather as the consequence of innovation: Firms' dynamic capabilities to innovate shape competition.[2] Consequently, Schumpeterian competition implies that antitrust enforcers better account for the necessary innovation incentives which generate effective competition.

But antitrust agencies predominantly remain, still today, within an idealized model of perfect competition. For instance, the model leads antitrust agencies and influential voices to think that competition increases as the number of firms in a market increases, if certain market conditions are met—and consequently, the reduction of the number of firms cannot suggest anything but a reduction of the level of firms competing in that market. Exceptionally, antitrust authorities have already recognized

[1] See, more generally, Teece (2009); Callegari (2021); Burlamaqui & Kattel (2019); Hanusch & Pyka (2007); Cantner et al. (2005); Hanusch & Pyka (2006); Bresnaha et al. (2012).

[2] Teece (2009); Barney (2001).

that the number of firms in a given market and the level of competition (e.g., prices; output) are not necessarily inversely correlated, given scale economies and capacity restraints, as CK Telecom,[3] where the General Court of the European Union held that the elimination of a competitor was not sufficient to prove "the elimination of the important competitive constraints which the parties to the proposed concentration exerted upon each other," otherwise "any concentration resulting in a reduction from four to three operators would as a matter of principle be prohibited."

Moreover, the model of perfect competition is the cause of the antitrust agencies' suspicion and misunderstanding of the nature of market power. Market power arises whenever there is a "mark-up" between marginal cost and marginal price, and market power can only amount to non-competitive market outcomes. Antitrust enforcers inadequately discriminate between "monopoly rents"—namely, rents resulting from the naked exercise of market power–from "Schumpeterian rents"—entrepreneurial rents resulting from an innovative project's ex-post value greater than its ex-ante cost.[4] Despite a minority of cases—to be further detailed in this essay, antitrust agencies and discussions have mainly ignored dynamic capabilities, however essential to understanding Schumpeterian competition.[5]

Finally, and most importantly perhaps, the model of perfect competition infers that antitrust agencies often disparage the dynamic analysis inherent to the evolutionary process of competition and innovation. Instead, perfect competition suggests that antitrust agencies should reach a present-day perfect competition, thereby discounting innovation incentives and the longer-term evolutionary competition process. Nevertheless, the dynamic process of competition seems to trigger interests (b) after being seriously overlooked (a). Thus, there is an urgent need to implement the Schumpeterian competition into operationalizable antitrust rules for an innovation-based enforcement policy in an age of disruptive innovation.

[3] European Commission v. CK Telecoms UK Investments Ltd., Case C-376/20 P, 13 July 2023 (European Court of Justice).

[4] Teece (2018).

[5] Teece (2009); Barney (2001).

1 Schumpeterian Competition Underestimated

Abstract

Schumpeterian competition suggests that innovation drives competition, with firms' dynamic capabilities shaping the competitive landscape. Antitrust agencies often operate under a perfect competition model, which overlooks market power and innovation incentives. This model leads to misconceptions about market power and competition and can result in erroneous decisions. Schumpeterian competition emphasizes workable competition, promoting innovation and dynamic competition. Market power should not be equated with monopoly rents, and a balance must be struck between preventing anticompetitive behavior and promoting innovation-driven competition. Reforming antitrust laws to accommodate changing economic landscapes is ultimately necessary.

Any textbook on antitrust would start by describing the perfect competition model for which antitrust agencies allegedly need to reach through interventions.[6] Under perfect competition, all sellers in a neatly defined market sell homogeneous products so that consumers can perfectly switch at no cost from sellers to sellers. Also, each seller in the market remains exceedingly small so that any increase or decrease of its output has no consequence on the market—no seller is a price-maker, every seller remains a price-taker. Prices are set at a competitive level, meaning with no profit margin. The market efficiently allocates the resources at no cost, thereby sellers and buyers can redirect their strategies costlessly. There is perfect information among market participants. Each market participant is fully aware of competing alternatives and constantly exerts an effective competitive constraint thanks to the market's cost of entry or exit.[7] Because "market power also reduces efficiency,"[8] the model of perfect competition bears normative implications to tackle often any market power, albeit being the essential component to innovate and thus compete.

For instance, as the notion of the perfectly competitive price depends on the firms' average costs, antitrust may become exaggeratedly worried about prices charged below-average costs—namely, predatory pricing. Using complex econometric and theoretical models, predatory pricing

[6] Hovenkamp (2021:2–18).

[7] Samuelson (1970:433).

[8] Shepherd & Wilcox (1979:50–52).

theory developed with this idealized notion of average cost. However, antitrust agencies struggle in delineating the difference between an aggressively competitive price and a predatory price. This struggle led agencies and courts to make uncontestable mistakes, as illustrated by the 1967 case of Utah Pie.[9] In this case, the defendants were three retailers of frozen pies. Each had less than 20 percent of the market share. The plaintiff's market share was more than 50 percent. Fierce competition among the rivals led to prices falling, and the plaintiff was a profitable company. The complaint claimed that defendants sold pies in Salt Lake City at a lower price in this city than their prices charged in other cities. Despite the fierce price competition and the sheer rivalry between the defendants and the plaintiff, the Court considered that the defendants' prices were charged "below costs": They allegedly engaged in predatory pricing and violated the Clayton Act. The case's outcome favored the dominant player, led to a price increase—meaning, the harms to competition, innovation, and consumers were palatable following the Utah Pie judgment. This result derives from an idealized idea of "competitive price"—this price is neither "below cost" nor above cost. In a less extreme approach, in Brooke v. Williamson Tobacco,[10] the Supreme Court considered the ability of recouping monopoly profits in the future as an essential factor of anticompetitive predatory pricing. Despite predatory pricing cases are difficult to be brought, these rulings show that, with the unrealistic perfect competition model focused on a misguided price theory, antitrust agencies and courts may continue to sanction pro-competitive and pro-innovative conduct, thereby leading to distort competition and stifle innovation.

Excessive pricing, by its turn, is not cognizable as a monopolization offense in the United States. In the United Kingdom, there are condemnations of Pfizer and Flynn Pharm by the Competition and Markets Authority for "unfair" pricing of medicines used for treating epilepsy.[11] In Italy, Aspen Pharmacare received a fine by the Autorità Garante Della Concorrenza e Del Mercato, for excessively increasing the prices for a medicine used for treating cancer.[12]

[9] Utah Pie. Co. Continental Baking Co., 386 U.S. 685, 87 S.Ct. 1326 (1967).

[10] Brooke Grp. Ltd. v. Brown & Williamson Tobacco Corp., 509 U.S. 209, 224 (1993).

[11] See CMA's decision of July 21, 2022, Case C3/9742-13.

[12] See decision by the Italian competition authority of October 14, 2016, Case A480.

None of the assumptions under perfect competition carry an inch of realism, but most importantly, to use the perfect competition model as a benchmark model for antitrust interventions obfuscates the role of antitrust in promoting competition and innovation. Nevertheless, it is generally accepted that "like all scientific models, the model of perfect competition applies only imperfectly in the real world; nevertheless, it can be of great service to the antitrust policymaker in producing the consequences of a certain action or legal rule."[13] On the contrary, the perfect competition model is exceptionally unhealthy. Perfect competition is unworkable as it prevents firms from innovating and from reinventing themselves. Therefore, a model of "workable competition" which departs from the model of perfect competition is inevitable should antitrust agencies want to operate in the real world:

> As to directions in which to look for possible improvement in the future, it may be worth considering the possibility that technical progress may bring about still closer and more general substitution; and also that the increased use of specifications, and more widespread knowledge of them, may help to bring more of these substitutes, or price-insensitive quality differentials, within the range of moderate and price-sensitive differentials. This would increase the number of industries which, despite large-scale production, have the characteristics of fairly healthy and workable imperfect competition, rather than those of slightly-qualified monopoly. In such cases, one may hope that government need not assume the burden of doing something about every departure from the model of perfect competition.[14]

The concept of workable competition theorizes the need to recognize that imperfect competition is the source of technical progress—in other words, of innovation and competition. But the concept of workable competition only partially accounts for what Joseph Schumpeter described as the fundamental source of competition: Innovation thanks to imperfect (or "monopolistic") competition. Indeed, criticizing the "glaring weaknesses in the mechanism of perfect competition," Schumpeter was the first to scorn "much of the optimism that used to grace the practical implications of the theory of this mechanism passes out through the ivory

[13] Hovenkamp (2021:12).

[14] Clark (1940:256).

gate."[15] Describing innovation as the evolutionary "process of creative destruction," Schumpeter underscored the mismatch between the perfect competition model and real economic life and articulated why the perfect competition model precludes the very process of competition. He powerfully stated that "perfect competition is not only impossible but inferior, and has no title to being set up as a model of ideal efficiency."[16] This lack of any usefulness and desirability of the model of perfect competition derives from its anti-innovation implication:

> If we try to visualize how perfect competition works or would work in the process of creative destruction, [...] all the essential facts of that process are absent from the general schema of economic life that yields the traditional propositions about perfect competition [...] Perfect competition implies free entry into every industry [...] But perfectly free entry into a new field may make it impossible to enter it at all. The introduction of new methods of production and new commodities are hardly conceivable with perfect – perfectly prompt – competition from the start. And this means that the bulk of what we call economic progress is incompatible with it.[17]

The crucial notion of free entry (and exit) inherent to the model of perfect competition, although detached from reality, pervades the current antitrust enforcement. Indeed, as Hovenkamp explains, the notion of entry barriers currently embraced by antitrust agencies comes from the structuralist economist Joe S. Bain.[18] According to Bain, entry barriers measure "the extent to which, in the long run, established firms can elevate their selling prices above the minimal average costs of production and distribution" without "inducing potential entrants to enter the industry." This definition of supra-competitive prices charged thanks to first-mover advantage implies that economies of scale can qualify as barriers to entry. According to Bain's prevailing definition of entry barriers, the greater the scale economies, the greater the entry barriers are. The Schumpeterian insight that "free entry" means no entry at all cannot be clearer: According to the perfect competition model, firms must be of such small size to ensure no entry barrier that entry in a new market

[15] Schumpeter (1942:104).

[16] Schumpeter (1942:106).

[17] Schumpeter (1942:104).

[18] Hovenkamp (2021:33–34).

is effectively made impossible given the firms' lack of scale and dynamic capabilities.[19]

However flawed and inadequate to innovation-driven competition, Bain's notion of entry barriers is "written into the 2010 Horizontal Merger Guidelines" promulgated by the Justice Department's Antitrust Division and the Federal Trade Commission (FTC).[20] However, the 2010 Merger Guidelines are generally perceived as a significant improvement compared to previous thinking concerning the importance of efficiencies, the dynamic analysis of the market, and the necessary evolutionary approach underlying the Guidelines. Therefore, the fundamental notion of entry barrier in the 2010 Merger Guidelines deriving from the perfect competition model demonstrates the considerable need to implement Schumpeterian competition further. Unfortunately, this type of competition remains primarily overlooked in antitrust enforcement.

As perfect competition would preclude technological progress, only imperfect competition can allow for innovative business strategies to take place as a possibility to effectively out-compete rivals. Market power thus causes firms to innovate, which itself enables competition. This dynamic, evolutionary approach to the competition should be prioritized by antitrust agencies and in antitrust discussions.[21] However, until now, an innovation-based assessment occurred only in a minor part of cases. Authorities nowadays expressly affirm that dynamic effects and innovation must be considered. Most of their soft law, including guidelines they issue, acknowledge that. See, for instance, the newly published FTC and DOJ Merger Guidelines provide "Considerations for Innovation and Product Variety Competition."[22] Nevertheless, the predominant approach the document undertakes is that a reduction in the number of competitors and an increase of market power will likely stifle innovation, an understanding not accurate according to Schumpeterian antitrust. Likewise, the Vertical Merger Guidelines from the European Commission also stress that "rivalry between undertakings is an essential driver of economic efficiency, including dynamic efficiencies in the form of innovation. In its absence, the dominant undertaking will lack adequate incentives to

[19] Teece (2009).

[20] Hovenkamp (2021:34–35).

[21] Ellig & Lin (2001).

[22] United States (2023).

continue to create and pass on efficiency gains." The European Commission's Horizontal Guidelines, by its turn, state that the dynamicity of a given market, including the pace of innovation, should be taken into account when assessing market share and concentration levels.

In this sense, not all market power should be associated with monopoly rents. It can be a result of successful innovation (Schumpeter rents) or more efficiency (Ricardian rents).[23] These two forms of rents are pro-competitive and should not be of concern to competition authorities. They do not involve raising prices (or reducing output below) above the competitive level. Schumpeter rents relate to creating newer products, enlarging output. Investments have risks so investors expect to earn more than the cost of capital (otherwise investments would not be made). Ricardian rents refer to offer same quality, lower priced (or higher quality, same price) products than competitors. More efficient firms tend to profit by pricing lower (expanding output). Not every firm that is earning positive profits is a monopolist or a firm that is exercising market power. It can be a price-taker that is earning profit due to lower costs. Schumpeterian competition and the entrepreneurial rents necessary to innovation and competition.[24]

The understanding that market power and a dominant position are not per se unlawful is consolidated in many antitrust statutes (e.g., Sect. 2 of the Sherman Act; articles 101 and 102 of the Treaty on the Functioning of the European Union—"TFEU") and soft law (e.g., Vertical Block Exemption Regulation—"VBER"). Cases like Eastman Kodak,[25] Trinko[26] in the United States, and United Brands[27] and Hoffmann-La Roche[28] in Europe reverberate the reasoning that, absent an abusive, unlawful conduct, market power should not be condemned by itself. Additionally, however, authorities should bear in mind the relationship between market power and innovation. In Eastman Kodak, the US

[23] Lind & Walker (2003).

[24] Teece (2009).

[25] Kodak Co. v. Image Technical Services, Inc., 504 U.S. 451 (1992).

[26] Verizon Communications, Inc. v. Law Offices of Curtis V. Trinko, LLP, 540 US 398 (2003).

[27] United Brands Company and United Brands Continentaal BV v Commission of the European Communities. Chiquita Bananas. Case 27/76 (1978).

[28] Hoffmann-La Roche v. Commission, 1979 E.C.R. 461 (1979).

Supreme Court ruled against Kodak not because it had 100% of the relevant market, but because it adopted exclusionary action to maintain a monopoly without business justification. Similarly, in Hoffmann-La Roche, the European Court of Justice found that, in addition to its dominant position, the defendant had imposed agreements containing fidelity rebates in a way to harm competition. In United Brands, the European Court of Justice affirmed that "an undertaking's economic strength is not measured by its profitability (...) as large profits may be compatible with a situation where there is effective competition."

Baker writes that "seller market power is called monopoly power".[29] Drawing antitrust implications from a perfect competition model, it is thus stated that "monopoly power may be exercised on a range of competitive dimensions–most obviously by raising prices, but also, for example, by reducing quality or convenience, modifying product features, and altering the geographic locations and product niches served."[30] As antitrust discussions and enforcement remain largely "price-centric" rather than "innovation-centric," any price change by a firm with a reasonable market share becomes under antitrust suspicions of monopoly rents.[31]

Although the discussion on what antitrust policy's goals is not exactly new, the debate has indeed gained an unprecedented momentum lately, given the claims of market failures and the calls for an antitrust revolution with the rise of big tech companies. Neo-Brandeisians ponder that dominant position' power should be tackled as a standalone basis, regardless of the economic effects of mergers and practices in a given market. The acquisition of Wholefoods by Amazon in 2017, for instance, faced fierce opposition even though it involved no significant overlaps.[32] Similarly, the Staples-Essendant (2019), Microsoft-Linkedin (2016) mergers raised concerns to Neo-Brandesians not related to an economic-effects perspective. In the same sense, Sen. Elizabeth Warren called for the unwinding of several mergers involving highly innovative markets, including Amazon's

[29] Baker (2019:13).

[30] Baker (2019:13–14).

[31] Gilbert (2020).

[32] Klobuchar (2017); Sagers (2017).

acquisition of Zappos, Facebook's acquisitions of Instagram and WhatsApp, and Google's acquisitions of Waze, Nest, and DoubleClick.[33] Similarly, Lina Khan criticized the merger involving Amazon and Quidsi.[34]

Other decisions have shed light on authorities' intent to promote other values to their scrutiny instead of economic efficiency. In February 2019, the European Commission blocked the proposed acquisition of Siemens by Alstom, after concluding that the transaction would consolidate the two large players in the markets of (i) railway and metro signaling systems; and (ii) very high-speed trains. The European antitrust authority understood the deal would likely result in increase of prices, reduction of the output of products in the market, and could even stifle innovation. Contrary to the merging parties' allegations, the European Commission considered unlikely that non-European firms (e.g., located in China) could contest the parties' market power. The decision rose high controversy, given that the merger had the blessings of both German and French governments, which claimed that creating an "European champion" in the industry was necessary to compete against Chinese rivals. As a sign of protest, the German and French governments elaborated a joint manifesto requesting the reform of the European antitrust laws in a view to enable its flexibilization for contemplating interests related to industrial policy.

The proposal made by France and Germany highlights another aspect related to the scope of action of competition authorities that does not converge with the ideals of Neo-Brandeisians, nor aligns with Borkian antitrust. Differently from Brandeisians, which defends more antitrust intervention through deconcentration, the claims for European champions advocate for a lower level of antitrust intervention, so that protection of competition and of the consumer welfare are shunned in favor of fostering local industrial policy.

Neo-Brandeisians themselves have articulated a manifesto-like document. Responding to criticism on their lack of proposals to objectively reform antitrust rules according to their beliefs, leading Neo-Brandeisians, including, Wu, Khan, and Marshall Steinbaum, issued the "Utah Statement." Commenting on the statement, Devlin lists the following proposals by the Neo-Brandeisians scholars:

[33] Abbruzzese (2019).

[34] Khan (2017:768).

1. "Vertical coercion, vertical restraints, and vertical mergers should enjoy no presumption of benefit to the public;
2. By rule of statute, non-compete agreements should be made presumptively unlawful;
3. The Trinko doctrine of implied regulatory preemption should be overruled;
4. The Brooke Group for predatory pricing and Weyerhaeuser test for predatory bidding should be overruled;
5. The Berkley [sic] Photo standard for establishing monopoly leveraging should be restored;
6. The essential facilities doctrine should be reinvigorated for dominant firms that deny access to critical infrastructural services;
7. Structural presumptions should be restored;
8. The LinkLine doctrine holding that price squeeze allegations fail as standalone Sect. 2 claims should be overruled;
9. Noerr-Perrington should be overruled and replaced by a First Amendment defense and appropriate statutory protections for workers; and
10. The Clayton Act's worker exemption should be extended to all who labor for a living, regardless of statutory employment status, for horizontal coordination, collective bargaining, and collective action in service of either."[35]

Therefore, although we cannot categorically say that Schumpeterian competition has been completely ignored by antitrust enforcers, such a line of thinking should be urgently placed in the centrum of competition agencies' scrutiny. Innovation and its role in competition need to be considered as the main character of the competitive assessment, instead of playing only a marginal role.

2 Schumpeterian Competition Recognized

Abstract
Antitrust discussions are shifting toward a dynamic view of competition, focusing on fostering innovation in addition to traditional price-centric approaches. Scholars like Herbert Hovenkamp emphasize the

[35] Devlin (2021 176–177).

importance of considering innovation concerns in antitrust policy, as market dynamics change when innovation is introduced. Schumpeterian competition, driven by innovation, is gaining traction in antitrust debates, as scholars argue that traditional models of static price competition do not effectively address the complexities of innovation in today's markets. The Antitrust Modernization Committee recognizes the importance of innovation in rethinking antitrust enforcement but suggests adjustments to align antitrust policy with dynamic efficiency theories and prioritize Schumpeterian competition in competitive assessments. Recent cases, such as Monsanto's acquisition by Bayer, and Comcast-NBC Universal merger, illustrate the growing focus on innovation in antitrust enforcement. A balance needs to be struck between preventing anticompetitive behavior and promoting innovation-driven competition.

Antitrust discussions have nevertheless somehow started to re-discover the Schumpeterian insights: a dynamic view of competition not only better reflects market realities but also better steers antitrust enforcement in a pro-innovation pro-competitive way.[36] In other words, following the footsteps of Gilbert, who has been advocating for a shift away from price-centric antitrust to innovation-centric antitrust since approximately 1995, antitrust debates have increasingly accounted for the need to foster dynamic competition in the long term rather than forcing static competition in the short term.[37]

For instance, leading antitrust law scholars such as Herbert Hovenkamp started to write in the 2000s about the entirely different picture the introduction of innovation concerns would bring to antitrust policy. In 2005 he indeed wrote that:

> Speaking very generally, one would describe the market circumstances that facilitates price competition as several firms in the market, unrestricted entry, product homogeneity, good information held by both producers and consumers, and strong rules against price-fixing. But as soon as innovation is thrown into the mix, the story becomes more complicated. Innovation – and also intellectual property laws that protect it –can produce market power, and even monopoly in extreme cases. Furthermore, the set of market structures that produces aggressive price competition is often quite different from the structures that encourage significant innovation.

[36] Rubinfeld & Hoven (2001).

[37] Id.

> Much, perhaps most, profitable innovation occurs in relatively concentrated markets with a relatively small number of firms producing distinguishable products.[38]

The same year, Michael Katz and Howard Shelanski published a paper titled "'Schumpeterian' Competition and Antitrust Policy in High." They describe how static considerations become less relevant for antitrust agencies whenever a Schumpeterian type of competition (i.e., innovation-driven rivalry) occurs.[39] The authors discuss an "important movement in contemporary antitrust thinking, the Schumpeterian School." Almost two decades later, such a school is still in waiting in antitrust enforcement. Katz & Shelanski explain the challenges to antitrust raised by Schumpeterian competition. They consider that the prevailing models of static price competition fail to adequately address innovation concerns: "The theory and data that support the systematic presumption in favor of increased competition for purposes of static pricing and output efficiency thus have no analog when it comes to an understanding the optimal conditions for innovation."[40] They consider that Schumpeterians are right about shifting focus from static competition and presumptions that increased market power and market concentration inevitably lead to anticompetitive outcomes. They nevertheless consider that Schumpeterian insights do not warrant a radical antitrust retreat: Antitrust analysis needs an update, but there is no justification that antitrust is presumptively inappropriate. Instead, they call for antitrust enforcement "to refine its tools to account for and promote technological innovation more effectively through a fact-intensive and multi-dimensional analysis."[41] We propose such refinement below.

Also, the Antitrust Modernization Committee of 2007 recognized the importance of innovation and the challenge it brings in rethinking antitrust enforcement, but considered that current antitrust rules allow for sufficient flexibility to adjust antitrust in favor of innovation concerns: "[C]urrent antitrust analysis has a sufficient grounding in economics and is sufficiently flexible to reach appropriate conclusions in matters

[38] Hovenkamp (2005:14).

[39] Katz & Shelanski (2005).

[40] Katz & Shelanksi (2005:17).

[41] Katz & Shelanski (2005:20).

involving industries in which innovation, intellectual property, and technological change are central features."[42] Antitrust policy disposes already of vast economic and legal foundation that should be entirely disregarded. However, it needs adjustments in order to properly contemplate dynamic efficiency theories and to place Schumpeterian competition in the center of the stage of the competitive assessment.

In a rare article for antitrust law scholars, Herbert Hovenkamp scrutinized the antitrust implications of Schumpeterian competition and considers that "Schumpeter was correct that over the long run the gains from innovation dwarf the gains from government intervention to make the economy more competitive under the traditional criteria of price and output."[43] He noted that "In the short run, a practice may destroy a rival, produce monopoly, and may even appear to impair consumer welfare. But in the longer run, it may be part of the very process of creative destruction that Schumpeter believed to be the bedrock of economic progress."[44] Because harm to long-run innovation capabilities supposedly create more harm than harm to short-run price competition, Hovenkamp frames the relevant question for antitrust agencies in the following way: "When is an antitrust violation more likely to be innovation enhancing rather than innovation restraining?" In other words, among possibly identified antitrust violations, when should an antitrust violation be exempted because the long-run economic (consumer and innovation) benefits outweigh the short-run economic disadvantages?

The debate acknowledged that high-technology markets (or "innovation markets" as Gilbert put it[45]) poorly fit within the antitrust's prevalent model of perfect competition: Market dynamics and capital-intensive technologies suggest that competition take place on innovativeness rather than mere price competitiveness.[46] As scholars and enforcers were increasingly "looking for Mr. Schumpeter,"[47] noticeable improvements in both the antitrust debates and the antitrust enforcement.[48] For instance,

[42] Antitrust Modernization Commission (2007:38).

[43] Hovenkamp (2008:10).

[44] Hovenkamp (2008:3).

[45] Gilbert (2020).

[46] Lenard (2011); Crandall & Jackson (2011).

[47] Gilbert (2006).

[48] Rubinfeld & Hoven (2001).

antitrust agencies and scholars have increasingly addressed the complex relationship between competition and innovation, focusing on innovation incentives from a dynamic perspective.[49]

Most importantly, antitrust courts started to re-discover Schumpeter, as illustrated by the seminal case of Microsoft where the court declared:

> In technologically dynamic markets, however, such entrenchment may be temporary, because innovation may alter the field altogether. See Joseph A. Schumpeter, CAPITALISM, SOCIALISM, AND DEMOCRACY 81-90 (Harper Perennial 1976) (1942). Rapid technological change leads to markets in which "firms compete through innovation for temporary market dominance, from which they may be displaced by the next wave of product advancements." Shelanski & Sidak, at 11-12 (discussing Schumpeterian competition, which proceeds "sequentially over time rather than simultaneously across a market"). Microsoft argues that the operating system market is just such a market.[50]

The court subsequently considered that:

> We note that there is no consensus among commentators on the question of whether, and to what extent, current monopolization doctrine should be amended to account for competition in technologically dynamic markets characterized by net-work effects. [...] Indeed, there is some suggestion that the economic consequences of network effects and technological dynamism act to offset one another, thereby making it difficult to formulate categorical antitrust rules absent a particularized analysis of a given market.[51] (references omitted)

Furthermore, recent, seminal cases have shown that authorities have emphasized the role of innovation and dynamic effects in general. Although occasional, this type of analysis should be encouraged and should become the rule, rather than the exception.

Monsanto's acquisition by Bayer in 2018 is a seminal case in this regard. The German-based company acquired the US-headquartered firm in a $63 billion global transaction that involved several business segments in the agricultural sector, including crop protection (e.g., pesticides),

[49] Ellig (2001).

[50] United States v. Microsoft (D.C. Cir. 2001) 253 F.3d 34, 49.

[51] Id.

seeds (e.g., vegetable; cotton) and traits, and "digital agriculture." The case went under scrutiny from several antitrust authorities worldwide and it was approved in most countries conditioned to structural remedies, whereby the parties had to divest intellectual property and research capabilities, including R&D projects.

With respect to horizontal effects, the European Commission used a "four layer competitive assessment" to review the "(a) product/price competition between actual products of the Parties; (b) product/price competition between actual and forthcoming products or between forthcoming products of the Parties; (c) innovation competition including in particular the incentives to discontinue, delay or reorient ongoing pipeline projects; and (d) innovation competition including in particular the incentives to innovate in the future." The European Commission gathered patent data and found that the parties competed fiercely for research, discovery, and for developing pipeline projects targeting similar product markets and that the barriers to build R&D capabilities were very high. After conducting an in-depth review, which involved the analysis of more than 2,000 relevant product markets, the European Commission found that both Bayer and Monsanto were important innovators in the industry, and that merger as notified would have significantly reduced competition on price and innovation in several of such markets.[52]

Likewise, the DOJ's Antitrust Division found in the United States that, "[i]n addition to anticompetitive effects in each of the product markets resulting from the loss of head-to-head competition or vertical foreclosure, the Complaint also alleges that the merger would have a significant impact on innovation."[53] For instance, the DOJ concluded that, without the merger, competition between the merging parties across the genetically modified ("GM") trait markets would likely increase in the future. Bayer and Monsanto had new traits in their research pipeline that would render new pesticides to treat different crops, and farmers (clients) would benefit from the development of such innovations. The Bayer-Monsanto transaction occurred within a context of big mergers in the industry, such as DowDupont and ChemChina-Syngenta mergers, which also involved assessing dynamic effects and innovation.

[52] Case M.8084.

[53] U.S. v. Bayer AG, et al. (D.D.C. 2019).

Another example is Comcast-NBC Universal, a vertical merger involving the United States' largest video programming distributor (Comcast) and the owner of several cable programming networks (NBC). The DOJ's complaint alleged that Comcast's competitors need access to NBC's programming, including the NBC broadcast network, to effectively compete in the market, and that the merger as notified would reduce NBC's incentives to distribute its products to Comcast's rivals. According to the DOJ, this lack of incentives would harm innovation, given it would lead to less product offerings to consumers. The merger was approved conditioned to commitments undertaken by the merging parties, whereby they agree to license programming to online competitors to Comcast's cable TV services, subject themselves to anti-retaliation provisions and adhere to Open Internet requirements. According to the DOJ, the commitments "imposed will maintain an open and fair marketplace while at the same time allow the innovative aspects of the transaction to go forward."[54]

In Northrop Grumman-Orbital ATK, the FTC brought a complaint against the acquisition of Orbital ATK, Inc., by Northrop Grumman, companies engaged in the research, development, and manufacture of missile systems and solid rocket motors ("SRMs"). The case was seen as particularly sensitive, considering that Northrop was considered as one of the four companies capable of supplying the US Government with missile systems, including tactical missiles, strategic missiles, and missile defense interceptors. According to the FTC, the transaction would give the merged entity incentives and ability to discriminate competitors and harm innovation "for present and future missile system programs." The merger was approved through a consent agreement that imposed behavioral obligations on the merging parties, including making their products available to competitors on a non-discriminatory basis.[55]

More recently, dynamic effects were considered in other two vertical mergers, NVIDIA-Arm and Lockheed-Aerojet. In the first, the FTC sued US semiconductor chip supplier Nvidia Corp.'s $40 billion acquisition of UK-based semiconductor design firm Arm Ltd. As one of the main theories of harm of the case, the FTC found that the proposed acquisition

[54] United States (2011).

[55] See complaint in the matter of Northrop Grumman Corporation, and Orbital ATK, Inc., Docket No. C-4652, brought on June 5, 2018.

would have "the chilling effect on innovation induced by the combined firm's access to its rivals' competitively sensitive information supplied to Arm, and the combined firm's ability and incentive to stifle innovations that are unfriendly to its business interests."[56] In the latter, the Federal Trade Commission brought a lawsuit to block Lockheed Martin Corporation's $4.4 billion proposed vertical acquisition of Aerojet Rocketdyne Holdings Inc., the last independent US supplier of missile propulsion systems. According to the FTC, Aerojet collaborated closely and shared innovative ideas with its major clients, in addition to investing its own resources in R&D to support certain missile programs. With the transaction, the FTC understood that the merged entity would "no longer possess the same incentives with respect to R&D," considering that before Aerojet invested in technologies that it expected would yield the most benefits to its business, regardless of the identity of the prime contractor, and post-transaction they would "earn more if Lockheed wins the prime contract." In both cases the merging parties abandoned the deal after the antitrust authority raised its concerns.[57]

On the spectrum of conduct investigations, refusing to supply is among the conducts where the trade-off between static vis-à-vis dynamic efficiencies plays the most important role. This is because when authorities broadly intervene in order to impose the obligation on a firm to supply a certain product to companies in the downstream market, this reduces incentives for upstream firms to innovate by creating newer products in the first place. Therefore, assessing refusal to supply through a static competition lenses improperly disregards the effects of dynamic competition in the long run. The benefits of innovation in the long run should be put in front in detriment of short-run, static efficiencies. Unfortunately, the consideration of dynamic, long-term effects on refusal to supply cases have been analyzed only in a handful cases, such as Oscar Bronner v. Mediaprint[58] and Magill[59] in Europe.

[56] See complaint in the matter of Nvidia Corporation, Softbank Group Corporation, and Arm, Ltd., Docket No. 9404, brought on December 2, 2021.

[57] See complaint in the matter of Lockheed Martin Corporation, and Aerojet Rocketdyne Holdings, Inc., Docket No. 9405, brought on January 25, 2022.

[58] Oscar Brönner v. Mediaprint, Case C-7/97, [1999], CMLR 4 112.

[59] Radio Telefis Eireann v. Commission, Case 76-77R, 91/98R [1989] ECR 1141, [1989] 4 CMLR 749.

The first case is emblematic in the sense that it must be proven that input to which access was denied to a competitor is indeed essential for the downstream to compete. In addition to the essentiality of the input, the European Court of Justice stated that it must also be shown that the input is incapable of being duplicated in the future, or that it could only be duplicated with great difficulty. In the case at hand, the European Court of Justice understood that there were no insurmountable barriers for the plaintiff to develop its own distribution system (the "input" that was being denied by the defendant), and dismissed the complaint. The Magill case brought the discussion on the obligation to license intellectual property rights. The controversy arose after three television broadcast companies from the Republic of Ireland and Northern Ireland prohibited the complainant (Magill) from publishing and selling a guide (magazine) detailing the channels' listings of such broadcasters. After years of judicial dispute, the Courts concluded that, given the broadcasters' dominant position, by refusing to disclose to Magill such channels' contents they had prevented the emergence of a new market, comprehended as the active that Magill was performing.

However, the recent populist techlash having reinvigorated Brandeisian antitrust and advocating for a return to antitrust before antitrust law & economics stifled the road toward a more Schumpeterian perspective antitrust agency. Brandeisian antitrust should not depart antitrust agencies to travel down that road as Schumpeterian competition constitutes a tangible improvement of antitrust law & economics to benefit prosperity and innovation.

3 Schumpeterian Competition Implemented

Abstract

Borkian idealists prioritize efficiency and verticalization, while Neo-Brandeisians emphasize the negative impact on competition. Critics of Bork argue that his antitrust policy overlooks dynamic competition, emphasizing long-run efficiency and innovation. On the other hand, Schumpeterian competition emphasizes long-run efficiency and innovation, cautioning against hasty conclusions about market inefficiency. Antitrust enforcement should prioritize a case-by-case approach, considering potential competition and long-term corporate capabilities. The rule of reason should be applied to balance economic analysis with legal considerations. Global coordination on antitrust rules seems to be an essential component to prevent competition distortion and promote innovation.

On the one hand, some might say that the Borkian idealists overstated the importance of efficiency rationales and underestimated the risk of certain practices harming competition, such as verticalization, as is the case of Neo-Brandeisians. On the other hand, Borkian antitrust should receive the credit for bringing "coherence to a policy that had little or none."[60] In this sense, it brought important contributions, including price theory tools that boosted a more rational antitrust analysis, a remarkable shift from the previous appetite of enforcers to fight size at the expense of social welfare.

Still, Bork's narrow views on the consumer welfare standard have proven to be inadequate, notably by overlooking dynamic competition. Nowadays, even scholars commonly framed as belonging to the Chicago School recognize that.[61] Dynamic competition demonstrates that mainly focusing on a static snapshot of market features (e.g., price) distorts the assessment of innovation, mainly by withdrawing the legitimacy of a firm's earning temporary market power as a result of its investments on innovation (e.g., R&D).

This does not mean, however, that his Neo-Brandeisian critics got the picture right. On the contrary, Neo-Brandeisians call for the revival of certain values that find no solid foundation in the analysis of economic effects, and that may deteriorate social welfare in the form of discouraging investments that lead to products and services with higher quality and lower prices to consumers.

Therefore, the need for reform in antitrust policy is not a debate exclusive to a particular school of thinking, nor it belongs solely to one political spectrum. Schumpeterian competition applied to antitrust would suggest a dynamic approach to antitrust enforcement. In other words, we need "dynamic antitrust," as opposed to "static antitrust" (which until now remained the predominant view). The consolidation of a dynamic approach framework shall attribute less importance to structuralism, including market shares and concentration analysis, but instead

[60] Devlin (2021).

[61] Id.

should make antitrust rely more on potential competition and corporate abilities to compete in the long run.[62]

Concerning general policy implications, Ellig & Lin consider that Schumpeterian competition leads to the following normative conclusions:

1. Aims for long-run efficiency
2. Allow rewards to entrepreneurship
3. Market power is not per se anticompetitive
4. Do not subsidize firms
5. Allow for dynamic considerations in regulations

With respect to aiming for long-run efficiency, the authors claim that "[c]ompetition is a process that takes time to reveal 'its true features and ultimate effects.' What may appear inefficient today (market power, monopoly, fluctuations) may be vital to achieving efficiency tomorrow. Because there is no way of knowing the ultimate effects of this process beforehand, caution is required." In our view, it is a consensus that merger control review involves, in essence, a prospective analysis of the effects of a proposed transaction in the market. Authorities must act by evaluating the likely effects that a merger will generate if implemented, vis-à-vis a counterfactual analysis. Moreover, it is known and understood in most jurisdictions that merger efficiencies must be considered to the extent they can outweigh alleged anticompetitive effects. Anyhow, despite the theoretical acceptance of the benefits that can arise from efficiencies, the fact is that authorities have rarely accepted efficiencies claims in merger control cases.[63] Therefore, efficiencies must be given a fairer credibility, given its likelihood of occurrence, and its legitimacy to improve competition and to increase consumer welfare. This understanding is in line with allowing rewards to entrepreneurship, since, according to Ellig & Lin, "[e]ntrepreneurship drives competition, but it is not a riskless activity [...] Reward usually come in the form of supranormal profits."

In relation to market power, they argue that "[f]irms with market power have potentially more resources to channel into discovering or implementing innovations. In addition, a firm possessing market power

[62] Fernandes (2022).

[63] OECD (2023:10).

today may have earned it through past innovation." As described previously in this book, corroborating this view, Justice Scalia pondered in Trinko[64] that charging temporary monopoly prices is what induces businesses to take risks and innovate:

> The opportunity to charge monopoly prices—at least for a short period—is what attracts "business acumen" in the first place; it induces risk taking that produces innovation and economic growth. To safeguard the incentive to innovate, the possession of monopoly power will not be found unlawful unless it is accompanied by an element of anticompetitive conduct.

Therefore, we agree that market power should be seen as a legit incentive for companies to pursue investing in innovation, and by no means should be presumably anticompetitive, as it sadly occurred in Alcoa,[65] when Justice Hand posited that the Sherman Act did not condone "good trusts" and condemn "bad" ones, but "it forbad all."

Moreover, we argue that the proper finding on when market power actually exists in a given market must rely on effects, instead of structuralism. In addition to the fragilities that may result from an overreliance on market definition, authorities should not over-rely on market share for a finding of a dominant position. The FTC and DOJ's draft Merger Guidelines submitted to public consultations on July 19, 2023, was heavily criticized in this regard by many scholars.[66] Fortunately, the final version incorporated adjustments in order to link dominance with "durable market power," which relates to the importance of assessing countervailing factors, such as entry barriers, instead of the previously suggested market share threshold of 30%.

Regarding the need to not subsidize firms, according to Ellig & Lin, "[f]irms that refuse to implement new production techniques, to adopt new types of organization, or to provide new products should feel the consequences of their actions." Protecting competition means not protecting competitors, as well as it means not protecting small, less efficient, or less innovative companies over big, more efficient, or more innovative companies.

[64] Verizon Communications, Inc. v. Law Offices of Curtis V. Trinko, LLP, 540 US 398 (2003).

[65] United States v. Aluminum Co. of America, 148 F.2d 416 (1945).

[66] Hovenkamp (2023); Sandford & Wong-Ervin (2024).

Finally, they state that Schumpeterian competition would allow for dynamic considerations in regulations. In their view, "[t]raditional monopoly regulation focuses on maintaining a predetermined rate of return in an effort to approximate the allocative efficiency of perfect competition. Schumpeterian competition, however, reveals a greater source of efficiency from the potential for new combinations and new processes. Thus, rate-of-return regulation and territorial monopoly privileges impede the pressures of creative destruction."[67]

I not only agree with such conclusions, but also suggest principles that should be followed by authorities in favor of adopting Schumpeterian antitrust. Principles of dynamic antitrust (i.e., innovation-based antitrust) need to be designed before being implemented by antitrust agencies and courts in specific cases.

I articulate a Schumpeterian approach to antitrust by outlining ten principles of dynamic antitrust, namely[68]:

1. Industry-level market investigations should be encouraged, in addition to defining relevant markets;
2. Provide more legal certainty for incentivize innovation and competition;
3. Precautionary approach should be limited, and ex-post intervention is more adequate for allowing innovation to thrive;
4. Rule of reason should be favored, instead of rigid, unfounded legal presumptions;
5. Innovative-based business practices must receive a legality presumption, and the burden to prove should rely on enforcers to prove otherwise;
6. Collusions are the most damaging conduct and should remain the focus of enforces, with the caveat that the rule of reason should apply, given joint ventures may generate benefits;
7. Merger review cases should encompass innovation effects rather than price effects more often;
8. Political meddling in antitrust cases in order to favor other values or other policies should be avoided;

[67] Ellig & Lin (2001:20–21).

[68] This section builds on Portuese (2021a).

9. Antitrust authorities should receive increasing independence and more regulatory power; and
10. More inter-jurisdictions coordination and global antitrust rules should be adopted.

First, the market definition remains the first and critical stage of antitrust analysis. It is a legal requirement in several statutes for finding an antitrust infringement. However, market definition rules insufficiently depict competitive constraints exerted by potential competitors, exaggerate the role of price as a determinant to competition, and over-estimate the effects of market structure on market outcomes.[69] Market definition also triggers the risk of defining markets overly narrow or overly broad, and both outcomes are not desirable. This problem is even more serious today, with the rise of platforms that innovate to provide a range of new services in a fast pace. With a fact-finding inquiry at the industry level rather than market level, market investigation is a tool that will provide a more accurate portrayal of the competitive constraints faced by a company while considering adjacent markets, potential competitors, and industry dynamics.[70] Therefore, market investigations must coexist with market definitions, which may be less important when assessing dynamic effects.[71]

Second, the importance of the rule of law deserves better protection: Stronger legal certainty protects innovation incentives. Consequently, a more predictable and more transparent regulatory framework would incentivize firms to innovate and thus compete. For instance, intellectual property ("IP") laws and their relations to antitrust deserve enhanced legal clarity. Otherwise, both fields of law may fail, either by over-protecting intellectual property holders (via intellectual property laws) or by protecting inefficient competitors (via antitrust law and enforcement). A Neo-Schumpeterian approach could contribute with this issue.[72] The rationale for "IP" laws is to restrict short-term competition with allocative, static efficiency losses to foster dynamic gains in the future, and Schumpeterian antitrust prioritizes dynamic gains over such allocative

[69] Pleatsikas & Teece (2001).

[70] Pleatsikas & Teece (2001).

[71] Portuese (2021a:11–13); OECD (2019:16).

[72] Portuese (2024).

inefficiency. Narrowing the scope of patents (to avoid deterring investments), and fostering the good faith aspects in FRAND commitments, allowing standard essential patent ("SEP") holders to seek injunction reliefs, as in Huawei v. ZTE,[73] would be useful measures.[74]

Likewise, the interplay between sector regulation and competition enforcement must be better aligned, otherwise there is the risk of increasing companies costs due to legal certainty and of making public policies less effective. The European Court of Justice decision in Slovak Telekom[75] acknowledged that a dominant firm did not refuse to supply an essential input, and that it had to give access to it according to sectoral regulation:

> By analogy with the Court of Justice's findings in paragraph 224 of the judgment of 14 October 2010, Deutsche Telekom v Commission (C-280/08 P, EU:C:2010:603), referred to in paragraph 117 of the judgment under appeal, it should be considered that a regulatory obligation can be relevant for the assessment of abusive conduct, for the purposes of Article 102 TFEU, on the part of a dominant undertaking that is subject to sectoral rules. In the context of the present case, while the obligation imposed on the appellant to give access to the local loop cannot relieve the Commission of the requirement of establishing that there is abuse within the meaning of Article 102 TFEU, by taking account in particular of the applicable case-law, the imposition of that obligation has the consequence that, during the entire infringement period taken into account in the present case, the appellant could not and did not actually refuse to give access to its local loop network.

Also, innovative behaviors require antitrust humility in sanctioning a novel practice never sanctioned previously: Firms need either exemption for demonstrable innovation or be subject to forward-looking behavioral remedies rather than backward-looking fines or divestitures. This principle has already been materialized on a few occasions, including in Microsoft but it has to be adopted more often, as the European Commission itself recognized that "[t]he fact that the Commission and the Union courts have not yet had the opportunity to rule specifically on certain conduct

[73] Case C-170/13, Huawei Technologies Co. Ltd v. ZTE Corp. and ZTE Deutschland GmbH [2015], EU:C:2015:477.

[74] Portuese (2024).

[75] Slovak Telekom a.s., v. European Commission, Case C-165/19 P (2021).

does not, in itself, prevent the Commission from imposing a fine."[76] In this precedent, although Microsoft was found to have infringed Article 102 of the TFEU, the European Commission did not impose fine, considering that "there is no Union decisional practice or case-law regarding whether a SEP holder, which has given a commitment to license that patent on FRAND [fair, reasonable, and non-discriminatory] terms and conditions, abuses a dominant position when it seeks and enforces an injunction on the basis of that SEP against a potential licensee that is not unwilling to enter into a licence agreement on FRAND terms and conditions; and (ii) national courts have reached diverging conclusions in this question."

Third, the case-by-case approach to competition matters proves imperative: Antitrust ought to remain a judicial matter where courts can weigh out beneficial and detrimental consequences of the envisaged conduct. The time-consuming critique ascribed to antitrust in courts undermines the accuracy of the judgment and the necessary access to a justice system that each firm is entitled to. Competition regulation with ex-ante rules derives from a precautionary approach. Many innovative, pro-competitive conducts may be caught within the ambit of such regulation at the expense of innovation and competition. Therefore, not only the specificities of each case must be deeply considered, but also the use of ex-ante regulation must be undermined in order to preserve the unique aspects of each conduct, with particular attention to its effects on innovation. Deeper understanding of the circumstances of each case requires more involvement (and not less) of experts.[77] Intensive fact-finding inquiries on a case-by-case basis need to be prioritized as it occurred in Brooke v. Williamson Tobacco,[78] where the Supreme Court considered the ability of recouping monopoly profits in the future as an essential factor of anticompetitive predatory pricing. Merely structural presumptions or emphasis on non-efficiency factors—as intended by Neo-Brandeisians should be discouraged.

Fourth, the rule of reason needs to be generalized: Per se illegality and per se legality prevent the rational, fact-finding scrutiny of the competitive and innovative effects of each conduct. The rule of reason best

[76] Case AT.39985 – Motorola, European Commission's decision of April 29, 2014.

[77] Ibáñez Colomo (2018).

[78] Brooke Grp. Ltd. v. Brown & Williamson Tobacco Corp., 509 U.S. 209, 224 (1993).

provides the legal basis for a balancing test whereby the economic analysis of antitrust is enhanced and no longer rigid, undisputable shortcuts. Although presumptions and analytical shortcuts are used in antitrust, not all presumptions are found in economics.[79] The rule of reason itself encompasses presumptions.[80] But radical, inflexible, legal presumptions increase the likelihood of economic errors.

Fifth, evidentiary standards need to be consistent with legal and economic theories: Standard of proof and burden of proof determine the probability of a decision to be economically detrimental. Statutes and case law prescribe that merger control is prospective in nature, and actual anticompetitive effects are not mandatory, being enough to demonstrate actual or potential effects. In that regard, the standard of proof still needs to require evidence of actual or potential harm to consumers given a reduction of innovation or the use of monopoly rents. Moreover, the burden of proof needs to lay with the enforcers: It should not be for companies to demonstrate the harmlessness of their conduct (otherwise innovation becomes subject to a precautionary logic) but enforcers to provide evidence of the harm likely harm of the scrutinized conduct. In this sense, the European Court of First Instance has already reversed the European Commission decision in Airtours,[81] understanding that "the Commission's assessment of the foreseeable reaction of smaller tour operators, potential competitors, consumers and hotel-owners was incorrect and that it underestimated their reaction as a countervailing force capable of counteracting the creation of a collective dominant position." The digital markets that have emerged in recent decades are one of the main targets of the Neo-Brandeisian interventionist agenda. According to these thinkers, the great market power possessed by certain digital platforms must be promptly demobilized. However, digital markets are also the ones that are more prone to abrupt and disruptive innovation.[82] In this sense, adopting a precautionary logic may stifle innovation. In fact, against Neo-Brandeisians' interests, the cost of Compliance with regulations is

[79] Posner (1977:13); Kalintiri (2020:1).

[80] Bork (1965b:781).

[81] EU Court of First Instance Decision on Case T-342/99, Airtours v Commission, ECR II-2585 (2002).

[82] Evans & Schmalensee (2005).

relatively higher for small and medium-sized companies, in comparison to larger firms.[83]

Sixth, enforcement efforts need to focus on the most damaging conduct by companies: Conspiracies between competitors to facilitate cartels and collusions. As rivals need to engage in aggressive competition to generate an innovation race, strategies to thwart such a state of competition require a vigorous antitrust enforcement policy. However, because some collaborations such as joint ventures may generate benefits subject to antitrust agencies' inquiry, the generalized rule of reason to antitrust matters should apply. Following this logic, the European Commission's Guidelines on the applicability of Article 101 of the TFEU to horizontal co-operation agreements recognize the legit benefits of certain agreements, including R&D agreements, and provides exemptions to illegal presumptions.

Seventh, merger cases need to integrate innovation effects rather than price effects more often, as it occurred in Bayer-Monsanto and Dow-DuPont. Although vertical and conglomerate mergers frequently deliver greater efficiencies and innovation benefits than an immediate reduction of competition, horizontal vergers, especially involving an incipient firm with promising competitive capabilities, deserve heightened scrutiny under current antitrust rules.[84]

Eighth, politicization of antitrust that falls outside the scope of economic values needs to be avoided to develop a rational, objective economic analysis of antitrust matters. If political meddling may seem inevitable, however, it should be minimized. In doing so, antitrust agencies need to be fully responsible for the enforcement policy, and the role of the courts in reviewing antitrust cases proves essential. Political positions aimed at overseeing antitrust agencies' work to steer this work in a fashion that suits short-term political interests instead of economics must be avoided.

Ninth, the independence of antitrust agencies deserves further strengthening via increased regulatory power. For instance, the FTC needs to be fully equipped with today's enforcement tools available to the DOJ's Antitrust Division. Moreover, the greater the independence antitrust agencies enjoy from the government, the more long-term

[83] Bradford (2023:138).

[84] Rubinfeld & Hoven (2001); Katz & Shelanski (2005).

perspective these agencies may embrace. The Directive ECN + proposed in 2017 in Europe follows this principle. The problem is not securing antitrust agencies more power—as Neo-Brandeisians also suggest—, but what they will do with such power. If enforcers follow the Schumpeterian competition orientation and have clear guidelines, more power would be desired to bolster innovation, without the fear of increasing enforcers' discretion.

Tenth, because competition is increasingly global and distortion of competition often results from other nations' strategic policies, global rules on antitrust need to be adopted. In that regard, a more robust coordination effort among antitrust agencies, although already existent (e.g., forums such as International Competition Network—"ICN" and the OECD), proves highly necessary, and needs to be advanced. Additionally, global rules at the World Trade Organization on antitrust matters may provide the necessary regulatory framework for nations not to distort competition and, whenever claims of this occurring, a dispute settlement mechanism where antitrust matters can be addressed. The adoption of global rules would decrease companies' compliance costs and would enable more effective R&D investments, fostering innovation.[85]

If implemented, these principles of dynamic antitrust would help design an antitrust enforcement policy more aligned with the Schumpeterian view of competition where firms compete dynamically via innovation, benefitting consumers. Enforcers would then focus on allowing innovation to thrive, protecting the "innovative process," instead on intervening on a basis to reduce the incentives to innovate.

Putting Schumpeterian competition into practice involves facing obstacles. Anyhow, although such implementation is not immune to challenges, some of the elements here discussed have already been applied by antitrust authorities worldwide to solve them, as discussed throughout this book, even if just occasionally. These initiatives need to be adopted more widely and systematically.[86] Modern econometric techniques could be used to quantify innovation claims and the lack of exact measurement should not play against the use of Schumpeterian competition. Assessing companies' technological, managerial, and financial capabilities for organic growth vis-à-vis growth via merger is an important element for telling a merger's

[85] Bradford (2023:138).

[86] Portuese (2022).

counterfactual scenario. Increase evidence searching, including analysis of parties' internal documents can also demonstrate R&D intentions and market entry intentions. Given the crucial importance of innovation in the economies, authorities should be cautions in intervening when the effects on incentives to innovate are in play. Differentiating specific situations and certain markets where innovation is more likely to occur in comparison to markets where their probability is more remote mitigates the need for over-intervention.

This work shows that the obstacles to adopting a Schumpeterian competition approach are surmountable, and that dynamic efficiency should be a priority in the antitrust agenda.

Conclusion: Another Future for Antitrust—Dynamic Antitrust

In the grand and expansive narrative of antitrust law and economics, we find ourselves at a crucial crossroads, where the story of Brandeisian antitrust is not even close to reaching its conclusion. In the wake of the revolutionary tremors that were triggered by Borkian antitrust, a fresh and exciting chapter is just waiting to be written. This chapter calls for a daring reimagining, a reinvention of the economic analysis of law, where the horizon is not just reached but expanded. This is a chapter that encourages a bold reimagining.

The dawn of a dynamic, Schumpeterian approach to competition beckons with fervent urgency, illuminating a path forward in the somewhat shadowy landscape of antitrust enforcement and scholarship. This approach is likely to be widely adopted in the near future. It is becoming abundantly clear that a paradigm shift is absolutely necessary as we move away from the well-known shores of Borkian antitrust and are drawn inexorably toward the rising tide of politicization that is characteristic of the Brandeisian approach. This is the time for dynamic antitrust, which is an approach that is pulsating with the vitality of innovation, to establish itself as the beacon of hope and direction in the muddled impasse that exists between the philosophies of Bork and Brandeis.

Embracing a Schumpeterian antitrust is not merely a transition; rather, it is a revolutionary movement, an impassioned crusade to redefine and elevate the very essence of antitrust law and economics. We are on the

A. Portuese, *The Battle for the Future of Antitrust*,
Palgrave Studies in Institutions, Economics and Law,
https://doi.org/10.1007/978-3-031-75794-5

verge of entering a new era that calls for not only change but also transformation. This transformation must be one that is deeply in tune with the ever-changing forces of market realities and the unyielding spirit of entrepreneurship. A collective awakening is being called for by this movement, which is a rallying cry to academics, policymakers, and practitioners alike, urging them to ignite the flames of research and intellectual exploration. It is possible for us to create a new alloy of economic thought by delving deeper into the rich tapestry of Schumpeterian antitrust. This new alloy has the potential to revolutionize the field of antitrust.

The message that is being conveyed by this clarion call is one that is not only unambiguous but also profound: the requirement that antitrust agencies and courts adopt a Schumpeterian approach with complete and utter commitment is not merely a suggestion but rather an urgent imperative. If we continue to be rooted in the populist currents of Brandesian antitrust, we run the risk of unleashing a whirlwind of consequences. These consequences have the potential to impose burdensome costs on consumers and to suffocate the very essence of innovation. This is not a path that we take lightly, but it is one that we embark upon with the knowledge that the Schumpeterian approach is not merely a choice but rather an unavoidable destiny, intricately woven into the fabric of market dynamics and the lifeblood of entrepreneurial endeavors.

Because we are both academics and those who are responsible for enforcing antitrust laws, the responsibility that rests on our shoulders is enormous. In order to successfully navigate this journey, we need to have wisdom, foresight, and a relentless pursuit of innovation. This is similar to how pioneers chart new territories. This new approach should be embraced with the zeal of revolutionaries, and the time has come for us to bring the principles of dynamic antitrust to the forefront of the conversation. In spite of the fact that it is fraught with difficulties and ambiguities, this journey is filled with the promise of a future that has been reshaped. An envisioned future in which antitrust law and economics do not merely adjust to the shifting currents, but rather set sail on a path that is audacious, visionary, and uncharted for the industry.

This Schumpeterian vision is not only reshaping the present, but we are also sculpting a future in which antitrust law and economics flourish in an environment that celebrates and nurtures competition and innovation in perfect harmony. This is what we are doing when we embrace this vision. To rise above the mundane and the conventional, and to embark on a journey that will redefine the boundaries of what is possible in the realm of antitrust, this is a call to action. This is a call to action. For the purpose of unlocking a future in which the principles of dynamic antitrust illuminate the path to prosperity, progress, and unparalleled innovation, let us join forces in this endeavor, forging ahead with determination and a shared vision.

References

Abdela, A. Steinbaum, M. 2018. 'The United States has a Market Concentration Problem. Reviewing Concentration Estimates in Antitrust Markets, 2000-Present,' Roosevelt Institute, September 2018, http://rooseveltwec.wpengine.com/publications/united-states-market-concentration-problem/.

Abbruzzese, J. 2019. 'Elizabeth Warren Calls to Break up Facebook, Google and Amazon,' March 8, 2019, NBC News, https://www.nbcnews.com/tech/tech-news/elizabeth-warren-calls-break-facebook-google-amazon-n980911.

Aghion, P. 2004. 'Growth and Development: A Schumpeterian Approach,' Annals of Economics and Finance, Vol.5:1–25.

Allensworth, R. 2016. 'The Commensurability Myth in Antitrust,' Vanderbilt Law Review, Vol.69(1):1–69.

Antitrust Modernization Commission. 2007. Report and Recommendations. April 2007, https://govinfo.library.unt.edu/amc/report_recommendation/amc_final_report.pdf.

Areeda, P. & Turner, D.F. 1978. Antitrust Law, Boston, MA: Little Brown & Co.

Atkinson, R.D. & Lage de Sousa, F. 2021. 'No, Monopoly Has Not Grown,' ITIF Report, June 7, 2021, https://itif.org/publications/2021/06/07/no-monopoly-has-not-grown.

Ayal, A. 2014. Fairness in Antitrust: Protecting the Strong from the Weak. Hart Studies in Competition Law, United Kingdom: Bloomsbury Publishing.

Baker, J.B. 1989. 'Recent Developments in Economics That Challenge Chicago School Views,' Antitrust Law Journal, 58:645–655.

Baker, J.B. 2019. The Antitrust Paradigm. Restoring a Competitive Economy, Cambridge: Harvard University Press.

A. Portuese, *The Battle for the Future of Antitrust*, Palgrave Studies in Institutions, Economics and Law, https://doi.org/10.1007/978-3-031-75794-5

Barney, J.B. 2001. Competence Explanations of Economic Profits in Strategic Management: Some Policy Implications. In Jerry Ellig (Ed.) Dynamic Competition and Public Policy. Technology, Innovation, and Antitrust Issues, Cambridge, MA: Cambridge University Press, 45–64.

Bernatt, M. 2022. Populism and Antitrust: The Illiberal Influence of Populist Government on the Competition Law System, Cambridge: Cambridge University Press.

Berk, G. 1994. Alternative Tracks: The Constitution of American Industrial Order, 1865–1917, Baltimore: The John Hopkins University Press.

Berk, G. 2009. Louis D. Brandeis and the Making of Regulated Competition, 1900–1932, Cambridge, MA: Cambridge University Press.

Block, W. 1977. 'Austrian Monopoly Theory–A Critique,' Journal of Libertarian Studies, Vol.1(4):271–279.

Block, W. 1994. 'Total Repeal of Antitrust Legislation: A Critique of Bork, Brozen, and Posner,' The Review of Austrian Economics, Vol.8:35–70.

Bork, R.H. 1965a. 'The Crisis in Antitrust,' Columbia Law Review, 65(3):363–376.

Bork, R.H. 1965b. 'The Rule of Reason and Per Se Concept: Price Fixing and Market Division,' Yale Law Journal, 74(5):775–847.

Bork, R.H. 1966a. 'Legislative Intent and the Policy of the Sherman Act,' Journal of Law & Economics, 9:7–48.

Bork, R.H. 1966b. 'The Rule of Reason and the Per Se Concept: Price Fixing and Market Division,' Yale Law Journal, 75(4):373–476.

Bork, R.H. 1977. Vertical Restraints: Schwinn Overruled, Supreme Court Review, 1977:171–192.

Bork, R.H. 1978. The Antitrust Paradox. A Policy at War with Itself, New York: Basic Books Inc.

Boudreaux, D.J. DiLorenzo, T.J. 1993. 'The Protectionist Roots of Antitrust,' The Review of Austrian Economics, Vol.6(2):81–96.

Bougette, P. Deschamps, M. Marty, F. 2015. 'When Economics Met Antitrust: The Second Chicago School and the Economization of Antitrust Law,' Enterprise & Society, 16(2):313–353.

Bradford, A. 2023. Digital Empires: The Global Battle to Regulate Technology, New York: Oxford University Press:

Brandeis, L.D. November 1, 1912. 'The Regulation of Competition Versus the Regulation of Monopoly,' Address to the Economic Club of New York.

Bresnashan, T.F. Greenstein, S. Henderson, R.M. 2012. Schumpeterian Competition and Diseconomies of Scope. Illustrations from the Histories of Microsoft and IBM. In Josh Lerner & Scott Stern (Eds.) The Rate and Direction of Inventive Activity Revisited, Chicago: University of Chicago Press.

Brown, C.G. 1987. 'Borkian Antitrust Economics and the Chicago-School: A Judicial Draining of America's Entrepreneurial Spirit,' Antitrust Law & Economics Review, 19:29–40.

Buck, K. 2020. 'The Third Way, House Judiciary Committee, Subcommittee on Antitrust,' Commercial and Administrative Law, https://buck.house.gov/sites/buck.house.gov/files/wysiwyg_uploaded/Buck%20Report.pdf.

Burlamaqui, L. & Kattel, R. 2019. Schumpeter's Capitalism Socialism and Democracy. A Twenty-First-Century Agenda. (Ed.) Routledge Studies in the History of Economics, Oxon, UK: Routledge

Callegari, B. 2021. Foundations of Post-Schumpeterian Economics. Innovation, Institutions and Finance. Routledge Frontiers of Political Economy. Oxon, UK: Routledge.

Cantner, U. Dinopoulos, E. Lanzillotti, R.F. Entrepreneurship, the New Economy and Public Policy. Schumpeterian Perspectives. (Eds.) Heidelberg, Germany: Springer.

Chandler, A.D. Jr. 1990. Scale and Scope. The Dynamics of Industrial Capitalism, Cambridge, MA: Harvard University Press.

Chopra, R. Khan, L.M. 2020. 'The Case for "Unfair Methods of Competition" Rulemaking,' The University of Chicago Law Review, Vol.87:357–357.

Clark, J.M. 1940. 'Toward a Concept of Workable Competition,' American Economic Review, Vol.30(2):241–256.

Crandall, R.W. & Jackson, C.L. 2011. 'Antitrust in high-tech industries,' Review of Industrial Organization, Vol.18:319–362.

Crane, D. 2008. 'Technocracy and Antitrust,' Cardozo Legal Studies Research Paper No. 208, Texas Law Review, Vol.86.

Crane, D. 2014. 'The Tempting of Antitrust: Robert Bork and The Goals of Antitrust Policy,' The Antitrust Journal, Vol.79:835–853.

Crane, D. 2018. 'Antitrust's Unconventional Politics. Regulation,' Vol.41(2):18–22.

Crane, D. 2019. 'How Much Brandeis Do the Neo-Brandeisians Want?' The Antitrust Bulletin, 64(4):531–539.

Crane, D. 2020. 'Fascism and Monopoly,' Michigan Law Review, Vol.118(7):1315–1370.

DiLorenzo, T.J. & High, J.C. 1988. 'Antitrust and Competition, Historically Considered,' Economic Inquiry, Vol.26(3):423–435.

Devlin, A. 2021. Reforming Antitrust, Cambridge, United Kingdom; New York, NY: Cambridge University Press.

Dibadj, R. 2004. 'Saving Antitrust,' University of Colorado Law Review, 75:749–772.

Elhauge, E. 2018. 'Where is Antitrust Policy Going? An Interview with Einer Elhauge (Harvard Law School and John Briggs (Axinn),' 6th Bill Kovacic Antitrust Salon: Where is Antitrust Policy Going? Concurrences, September

14, 2018, https://www.concurrences.com/IMG/pdf/gwu_2018_-_speakers_interviews.pdf?54267/e1c062016b68dc04788f5b88dffc295cbadf78ef.
Ellig, J. 2001 (Ed.). Dynamic Competition and Public Policy. Technology, Innovation, and Antitrust Issues, Cambridge, UK: Cambridge University Press.
Ellig, J. & Lin, D. 2001. A Taxonomy of Dynamic Competition Theories. In Jerry Ellig (Ed.) Dynamic Competition and Public Policy. Technology, Innovation, and Antitrust Issues, Cambridge, MA: Cambridge University Press, 16–44.
Evans, D. & Padilla, J. 2005. 'Designing Antitrust Rules for Assessing Unilateral Practices: A Neo-Chicago Approach,' University of Chicago Law Review, 72:76–80.
Evans, D. & Schmalensee, R. 2001. Some Economic Aspects of Antitrust Analysis in Dynamically Competitive Industries, NBER Working Paper No. w8268, May 5, 2001, https://papers.ssrn.com/sol3/papers.cfm?abstract_id=268877.
Ezrachi, A. 2016. 'Sponge,' Journal of Antitrust Enforcement, Vol.5(1):49–75.
Felice, F. & Vatiero, M. 2014. 'Ordo and European Competition Law,' Research in the History of Economic Thought and Methodology, Vol.32:147–157.
Flynn, J.J. 1977. 'Antitrust Jurisprudence: A Symposium on the Economic, Political and Social Goals of Antitrust Policy,' University of Pennsylvania Law Review, Vol.125(6):1182–1190.
Foge, Z. 2019. 'American Oligarchy: How the Enfeebling of Antitrust Law Corrodes The Republic,' The Journal of Business, Entrepreneurship & the Law, Vol.12(1):119–148.
Foran, C. 2017. Democrats Bet on a Populist Message to Win Back Congress, The Atlantic, July 24, 2017, https://www.theatlantic.com/politics/archive/2017/07/democrats-message-populist-monopolies-congress-trump/534603/.
Fox, E. 1981. 'The Modernization of Antitrust: A New Equilibrium,' Cornell Law Review, 66:1140–1192.
Fox, E. 2022. 'A Wider Lens: Neo-Brandeis and Ordoliberalism as Alternative Narratives that Liberate a Antitrust Thinking in the Developing World,' Thirteen Session of the UNCTAD Research Partnership Platform Intergovernmental Group of Experts, July 20, 2023, https://unctad.org/system/files/non-official-document/ccpb_RPP_presentation_Fox_en.pdf.
Ganapati, S. 2020. 'Growing Oligopolies, Prices, Output, and Productivity?' American Economic Journal (forthcoming), https://scholar.google.com/scholar_url?url=https://www.sganapati.com/files/Ganapati_2019_OligopoliesPricesQuantities_AEJmicro.pdf&hl=en&sa=T&oi=gsb-gga&ct=res&cd=0&d=7336776682706576318&ei=dfm9YJrGBYWVy9YP7pOngAU&scisig=AAGBfm3Vbjx_LWKXqf9WbmteCjSYc4cdSg.

Gilbert, R. 2006. Looking for Mr. Schumpeter: Where Are We in the Competition-Innovation Debate? In Jaffre, A.B. et al. (Eds.) Innovation Policy and the Economy, Cambridge, MA: MIT Press, 159–215.

Gilbert, R.J. 2020. Innovation Matters. Competition Policy for the High-Technology Economy, Cambridge, MA: MIT Press.

Goldfein, S. Keyte, J. 2017. ''A Better Deal' on Antitrust Enforcement: Can Democrats Catch the Populist Wave?' New York Law Journal, Vol.258(26), August, 8, 2017, https://www.skadden.com/-/media/files/publications/2017/08/abetterdealonantitrustenforcementcandemocratscatch.pdf.

Grandy, C. 2009. 'Original Intent and the Sherman Antitrust Act: A Re-examination of the Consumer-Welfare Hypothesis,' Journal of Economic History, Vol.53(2):359–376.

Grullon, G. Larkin, Y. Michaely, R. 2019. 'Are US Industries Becoming More Concentrated?' Review of Finance, 697–743.

Hanusch, H. & Pyka, A. 2006. 'Principles of Neo-Schumpeterian Economics,' Cambridge Journal of Economics, Vol.31:275–289.

Hanusch, H. & Pyka, A. 2007. Elgar Companion to Neo-Schumpeterian Economics, Cheltenham, UK: Edward Elgar.

Hart, D.M. 2001. 'Antitrust and Technological Innovation in the US: Ideas, Institutions, Decisions, and Impacts, 1890–2000,' Research Policy, Vol.30, 93–96.

Hawley, J. 2021a. The Tyranny of Big Tech, Washington D.C.: Regnery Publishing.

Hawley, J. 2021b. 'Senator Hawley Introduces the Bust Up Big Tech Act,' Hawley.senate.gov, April 19, 2021, https://www.hawley.senate.gov/senator-hawley-introduces-bust-big-tech-act.

Hesse, R. 2016. 'And Never the Twain Shall Meet? Connecting Popular and Professional Visions for Antitrust Enforcement. Acting Assistant Attorney General Renata Hesse of the Antitrust Division Delivers Opening Remarks at 2016 Global Antitrust Enforcement Symposium, Washington D.C., September 20, 2016, https://www.justice.gov/opa/speech/acting-assistant-attorney-general-renata-hesse-antitrust-division-delivers-opening.

Hien, J. 2023. 'The Rise and Fall of Ordoliberalism,' Socio-Economic Review, April 03, 2023, https://academic.oup.com/ser/advance-article/doi/https://doi.org/10.1093/ser/mwad018/7100859

High, J. 1984. 'Bork's Paradox: Static vs. Dynamic Efficiency in Antitrust Analysis,' Contemporary Policy Issues, Vol.3(2):21–34.

Hoffmann, L. Parisi, R. Serra, N. 2020. 'Hipster Antitrust and the Brazilian Legal System,' The Future of Antitrust, 2020: 21–33.

Hovenkamp, H. 2001. 'Post-Chicago Antitrust: A Review and Critique,' Columbia Business Law Review, 2001:257–337.

Hovenkamp, H. 2005. The Antitrust Enterprise. Principle and Execution, Cambridge: Harvard University Press.

Hovenkamp, H. 2008. 'Schumpeterian Competition and Antitrust,' Competition Policy International, November 1, 2008, 4:2–12.

Hovenkamp, H. 2018. 'Whatever Did Happen to the Antitrust Movement?' Notre Dame Law Review, 94(2):583–638.

Hovenkamp, H. 2019. 'Is Antitrust's Consumer Welfare Principle Imperiled?' The Journal of Corporation Law, 45(1):65–94.

Hovenkamp, H. 2021. Principles of Antitrust Law. 2nd Edition. St Paul, MN: West Academic Publishing.

Hovenkamp, H. 2024. 'The 2023 Merger Guidelines: Law, Fact, and Method,' January 11, 2024, https://papers.ssrn.com/sol3/papers.cfm?abstract_id=4684465.

Hubbard, S. 2020. Monopoly Sucks. 7 Ways Big Corporations Rule Your Life and How to Take Back Control, New York: Simon & Schuster.

Ibáñez Colomo, P. 2018. The Shaping of EU Competition Law, Cambridge: Cambridge University Press.

Jacobs, M. 1995. 'An Essay on the Normative Foundations of Antitrust Economics,' North Carolina Law Review, Vol.74(1):219–266.

Kalintiri, A. 2020. 'Analytical Shortcuts in EU Competition Enforcement: Proxies, Premises and Presuptions,' Journal of Competition Law and Economics, Vol.16(3):392–433.

Kang, C. 2021. Lawmakers, Taking Aim at Big Tech, Push Sweeping Overhaul of Antitrust, The New York Times, June 11, 2021, https://www.nytimes.com/2021/06/11/technology/big-tech-antitrust-bills.html.

Katz, M.L. Shelanski, H. 2006. ''Schumpeterian' Competition and Antitrust Policy in High-Tech Markets,' Competition, 14:1–20.

Kennedy, J. 2020. 'Are Markets Becoming More Concentrated?' ITIF Report, June 2020, https://itif.org/publications/2020/06/29/monopoly-myths-are-markets-becoming-more-concentrated.

Kessler, A. 2021. 'Unfortunately, 'Big Is Bad' Is Back,' Wall Street Journal, June 6, 2021, https://www.wsj.com/articles/unfortunately-big-is-bad-is-back-11622995107.

Khan, L. 2017. 'Amazon's Antitrust Paradox,' The Yale Law Journal, Vol.126:710–805.

Khan, L. & Vaheesan, S. 2017. 'Market Power and Inequality: The Antitrust Counterrevolution and Its Discontents,' Harvard Law & Policy Review, Vol.11(1):235–294.

Khan, L. 2018. 'The New Brandeis Movement: America's Antimonopoly Debate,' Journal of European Competition Law & Practice, 9(3):131–132.

Kirkwood, J.B. Lande, R.H. 2008a. 'The Fundamental Goal of Antitrust: Protecting Consumers, Not Increasing Efficiency,' Notre Dame Law Review, Vol.84:191–243.

Kirkwood, J.B. Lande, R.H. 2008b. The Chicago School's Foundation is Flawed: Antitrust Protects Consumers, In R. Pitofsky (Ed.) How the Chicago School Overshot the Mark: The Effect of Conservative Economic Analysis on U.S. Antitrust, Oxford: Oxford University Press, 89–106.

Klobuchar, A. 2017. 'Klobuchar Statement on FTC Approval of Amazon-WholeFoods Merger,' August 25, 2017, https://www.klobuchar.senate.gov/public/index.cfm/2017/8/klobuchar-statement-on-ftc-approval-of-amazon-whole-foods-merger.

Kishi, D. 'Robert Bork's America, The American Conservative, March 1, 2018, http://www.theamericanconservative.com/articles/robert-borks-america/.

Klobuchar, A. 2021. Antitrust. Taking on Monopoly Power from the Gilded Age to the Digital Age, New York: Alfred A. Knopf.

Kovacic, W. 1989. 'Failed Expectations: The Troubled Past and Uncertain Future of the Sherman Act as a Tool for Deconcentration,' Iowa Law Review, Vol.74:1105–1130.

Kovacic, W. 2007. 'The Intellectual DNA of Modern U.S. Competition Law for Dominant Firm Conduct: The Chicago/Harvard Double Helix,' Columbia Business Law Review, 1(1):1–80.

Lamadrid de Pablo, A. 2017. 'Competition Law as Fairness,' Journal of European Competition Law & Practice, Vol.8:147–148.

Lande, R.H. 1982. 'Wealth Transfers as the Original and Primary Concern of Antitrust: The Efficiency Interpretation Challenged,' Hastings Law Journal, Vol.34:65–151.

Lande, R.H. 1999. 'Proving the Obvious: The Antitrust Laws Were Passed to Protect Consumers (Not just to Increase Efficiency),' Hastings Law Journal, Vol.50:959–968.

Lenard, T.M. 2011. 'Introduction: Antitrust and the Dynamics of Competition in High-Tech Industries,' Review of Industrial Organizations, Vol.38:311–317.

Letwin, William. 1954. Law and Economic Policy in America. The Evolution of the Sherman Antitrust Act, Chicago: Chicago University Press [1981].

Lind, R; Walker, M. 2003. 'The (mis)use of profitability analysis in competition law cases,' CRA Competition Policy Discussion Paper 9, December, 2023, https://www.semanticscholar.org/paper/CRA-COMPETITION-POLICY-DISCUSSION-PAPERS-9-The-of/f34b12a49ae81e33b6238bcd54aab8eac40aeedf.

Lynn, B.C. 2010a. Cornered: The New Monopoly of Capitalism and the Economics of Destruction, Wiley.

Lynn, B.C. 2010b. 'Who Broke America's Jobs Machine?' Washington Monthly, March/April 2010.

Lynn, B.C. 2012. 'Killing the Competition,' Harper's Magazine, February 2012, https://harpers.org/archive/2012/02/killing-the-competition/.

Lynn, B.C. & Philipp Longman. 2016. 'Populism with a Brain,' Washington Monthly, June/July/August 2016, https://washingtonmonthly.com/magazine/junejulyaug-2016/populism-with-a-brain/.

Lynn, B.C. 2020. Liberty from All Masters: The New American Autocracy vs. the Will of the People, New York: St Martin's Press.

Matsurra, J.H. Jefferson vs. The Patent Trolls: A Populist Vision of Intellectual Property Rights, Charlottesville: University of Virginia Press.

Mossoff, A. 2007. 'Who Cares What Thomas Jefferson Thought About Patents—Reevaluating the Patent Privilege in Historical Context,' Cornell Law Review, Vol.92(5):953–1012.

Nadler, J. Cicilline, D.N. 2020. Investigation of Competition in Digital Markets. Majority Staff Report and Recommendations. Subcommittee on Antitrust, Commercial and Administrative Law of the Committee on the Judiciary, https://judiciary.house.gov/uploadedfiles/competition_in_digital_markets.pdf?utm_campaign=4493-519.

Nelson, P. & Smith, D. 2015. 'Efficiencies in Antitrust Analysis: A View from the Middle of the Road,' The Antitrust Bulletin, Vol.60 (2):128–149.

Open Markets Institute (2019) Petition for Rulemaking to Prohibit Worker Non-Compete Clauses, March 20, 2019, https://static1.squarespace.com/static/5e449c8c3ef68d752f3e70dc/t/5eaa04862ff52116d1dd04c1/1588200595775/Petition-for-Rulemaking-to-Prohibit-Worker-Non-Compete-Clauses.pdf.

Open Markets Institute (2020) Petition for Rulemaking to Prohibit Exclusionary Contracts, July 21, 2020, https://static1.squarespace.com/static/5e449c8c3ef68d752f3e70dc/t/5f1729603e615a270b537c3d/1595353441408/Petition+for+Rulemaking+to+Prohibit+Exclusionary+Contracts.pdf.

Orbach, B.Y. 2010. 'The Antitrust Consumer Welfare Paradox,' Journal of Competition Law & Economics, Vol.7(1):133–164.

Orbach, B.Y. 2017. 'Antitrust Populism,' N.Y.U. Journal of Law & Business, Vol.14(1):1–25.

Organisation for Economic Co-operation and Development. 2008. Dynamic Efficiencies in Merger Analysis, May 15, 2008, https://www.oecd.org/daf/competition/40623561.pdf.

Organisation for Economic Co-operation and Development. 2019. Merger Control in Dynamic Markets, December, 2019, https://web-archive.oecd.org/2020-03-10/546724-merger-control-in-dynamic-markets-2020.pdf.

Organisation for Economic Co-operation and Development. 2023. Out-of-Market Efficiencies in Competition Enforcement, December 6, 2023, https://www.oecd.org/daf/competition/out-of-market-efficiencies-in-competition-enforcement-2023.pdf.

Page, W.H. 'Ideological Conflict and the Origins of Antitrust Policy,' Tulane Law Review, Vol.66(1):1–67.

Paul, S. 'Antitrust as Allocator of Coordination Rights,' UCLA Law Review, 67:378–431.

Parisi, R. 2024. 'The Regulation of Competition in Brazil: Comments on the Digital Markets Law Bill (PL 2768/2022),' The George Washington Competition & Innovation Lab, January 6, 2024, https://www.gwucic.com/post/the-regulation-of-competition-in-brazil-comments-on-the-digital-markets-law-bill-pl-2768-2022-1.

Peritz, R.J. 1990. 'A Counter-History of Antitrust Law,' Duke Law Journal, Vol.1990:263–320.

Pitofsky, R. 1979. 'The Political Content of Antitrust,' University of Pennsylvania Law Review, Vol.127:1051–1075.

Pleatsikas, C. & Teece, D.J. 2001. New Indicia for Antitrust Analysis in Markets Experiencing Rapid Innovation. In Jerry Ellig (Ed.) Dynamic Competition and Public Policy. Technology, Innovation, and Antitrust Issues, Cambridge, MA: Cambridge University Press, 95–137.

Portuese, A. 2020a. 'Beyond Antitrust Populism: Towards Robust Antitrust,' Economic Affairs, 40(2):237–258.

Portuese, A. 2020b. European Competition Enforcement and the Digital Economy: The Birthplace of Precautionary Antitrust, in Global Antitrust Instituted (Ed.) Report on the Digital Economy, 597–651.

Portuese, A. 2021a. 'Principles of Dynamic Antitrust,' ITIF Report, June 14, 2021, Principles of Dynamic Antitrust: Competing Through Innovation, https://itif.org/publications/2021/06/14/principles-dynamic-antitrust-competing-through-innovation.

Portuese, A. 2021b. 'The Digital Markets Act: European Precautionary Antitrust,' ITIF Report, May 2021, https://itif.org/publications/2021/05/24/digital-markets-act-european-precautionary-antitrust.

Portuese, A. 2021c. Precautionary Antitrust: A Precautionary Tale in European Competition Policy. In M. Klaus & Tor, A. (Eds.) Law and Economics of Regulation. Economic Analysis of Law in European Legal Scholarship, Vol.11 Cham: Springer.

Portuese, A. 2022. 'Biden Antitrust: The Paradox of the New Antitrust Populism,' George Mason Law Review, Vol.29(4)1087–1133.

Portuese, A. 2023. 'Making Sense of EU Merger Control: The Need for Limiting Principles,' CPI Antitrust Chronicle, November 2023.

Portuese, A. 2024. 'Antitrust and Intellectual Property Rights: Toward a New Schumpeterian Approach,' The George Washington Competition & Innovation Lab, January 6, 2024, https://www.gwucic.com/post/antitrust-and-intellectual-property-rights-toward-a-new-schumpeterian-approach.

Posner, R. 1977. 'The Rule of Reason and the Economic Approach: Reflections on the Sylvania Decision,' University of Chicago Law Review, Vol.45:1–20.

Posner, R. 1979. 'The Chicago School of Antitrust Analysis,' University of Pennsylvania Law Review, Vol.127:925–948.

Posner, R. 2001. Antitrust Law. 2nd Edition, Chicago: University of Chicago Press.

Raj, P. 2017. 'Antimonopoly Is as Old as the Republic,' ProMarket, May 22, 2017, https://promarket.org/2017/05/22/antimonopoly-old-republic/.

Rubinfeld, D.L. & Hoven, J. 2001. Innovation and Antitrust Enforcement. In Jerry Ellig (Ed.) Dynamic Competition and Public Policy. Technology, Innovation, and Antitrust Issues, Cambridge, MA: Cambridge University Press, 65–94.

Samuelson, P. 1970. Economics. 7th Edition. New York: McGraw Hill.

Sandford, J., Wong-Ervin, K. 2024. 'New DOJ-FTC Merger Guidelines: Opportunities and Strategies for Merging Parties,' The George Washington Competition & Innovation Lab, January 6, 2024, https://www.gwucic.com/post/new-doj-ftc-merger-guidelines-opportunities-and-strategies-for-merging-parties-1.

Schmalensee, R. 2000. 'Antitrust Issues in Schumpeterian Industries,' American Economic Review, 90 (2):192–196.

Schumpeter, J.A. 1942. Capitalism, Socialism, and Democracy. 3rd Edition. New York: HarperPerennial [2008]

Sagers, C. 2017. 'Crack Down on Amazon,' Slate, June 19, 2017, https://perma.cc/7X7T-ZY3M.

Shapiro, C. 2018. 'Antitrust in a Time of Populism,' International Journal of Industrial Organization, Vol.61:714–748.

Sherman, J. 1895. John Sherman's Recollections of Forty Years in The House, Senate and Cabinet. An Autobiography, Vol.II, New York: The Werner Company.

Sherpherd, W.G. & Wilcox, C. 1979. Public Policies Toward Business, 6th Edition. Homeword, Ill: Richard D. Irwin Inc.

Sitaraman, G. 2018. 'Taking Antitrust Away from the Courts,' The Great Democracy Initiative, September 2018, https://greatdemocracyinitiative.org/wp-content/uploads/2018/09/Taking-Antitrust-Away-from-the-Courts-Report-092018-3.pdf.

Slaughter, R.K. 2021. Keynote Remarks of FTC Acting Chairwoman Rebecca Kelly Slaughter at the Consumer Federation of America's Virtual Consumer Assembly, May 4, 2021, https://www.ftc.gov/system/files/documents/pub

lic_statements/1589607/keynote-remarks-acting-chairwoman-rebecca-kelly-slaughte-cfa-virtual-consumer-assembly.pdf.
Solow, R. 1956. 'A Contribution to the Theory of Economic Growth,' Quarterly Journal of Economics, Vol.70(1):65–94.
Stein, J. 2017. Chuck Schumer just previewed Democrat's plan to take economic populism back from Trump, Vox, July 23, 2017, https://www.vox.com/2017/7/23/16016676/chuck-schumer-democrats-populism.
Stucke, M.E. 2009. 'Does the Rule of Reason Violate the Rule of Law?' U.C. Davis Law Review, Vol.259:1375–1490.
Sullivan, L.A. 1995. 'Post-Chicago Economics: Economists, Lawyers, Judges, and Enforcement in a Less Determinate Theoretical World,' Antitrust Law Journal, 63:669–681.
Teachout, Z. & Khan, L. 2014. 'Market Structure and Political Law: A Taxonomy of Power,' Duke Journal of Constitutional Law & Public Policy, Vol.9(1):37–74.
Teachout, Z. 2020. Break'Em Up: Recovering Our Freedom from Big Ag, Big Tech, and Big Money, New York: All Points Books.
Teece, D.J. 2009. Dynamic Capabilities & Strategic Management. Organizing for Innovation and Growth, Oxford: Oxford University Press.
Teece, D.J. 2018. Entrepreneurial Rents. In Augier, M. & Teece, D.J. (Eds.) The Palgrave Encyclopedia of Strategic Management, London: Macmillan Palgrave, 503–504.
Tracy, R. 2021. 'New York Senate Passes Antitrust Bill Targeting Tech Giants,' The Wall Street Journal, June 7, 2021, https://www.wsj.com/articles/new-york-senate-passes-antitrust-bill-targeting-tech-giants-11623098225.
United States, 2011. 'Justice Department Allows Comcast-NBCU Joint Venture to Proceed with Conditions,' U.S. Department of Justice, January 18, 2011, https://www.justice.gov/opa/pr/justice-department-allows-comcast-nbcu-joint-venture-proceed-conditions.
United States, 2018. Market Concentration—Note by the United States. Hearing on Market Concentration, OECD, June 7, 2018, https://one.oecd.org/document/DAF/COMP/WD(2018)59/en/pdf.
United States, 2023. 'Merger Guidelines', US Department of Justice and Federal Trade Commission, December 18, 2023, https://www.ftc.gov/system/files/ftc_gov/pdf/P234000-NEW-MERGER-GUIDELINES.pdf.
Vaheesan, S. 2014. 'The Evolving Populisms of Antitrust,' Nebraska Law Review, Vol.93:370–428.
Vatiero, M. 2015. 'Dominant Market Position and Ordoliberalism,' International Review of Economics, Vol.62(4):291–306.
Voorhees, T.Jr. 'The Political Hand in American Antitrust—Invisible, Inspirational, or Imaginary?' Antitrust Law Journal, Vol.79:557–576.

Werden, G. J. 2020. The Foundations of Antitrust. Events, Ideas, and Doctrines, Durham, NC: Carolina Academic Press.

Wu, T. 2018. The Curse of Bigness: Antitrust in the New Gilded Age, Columbia: Columbia Global Reports.

Wu, T. 2019. Antitrust and Competition Conference—Digital Platforms, Markets, and Democracy, Conference of the Stigler Center of the University of Chicago, https://www.youtube.com/watch?v=Y_Jp-GJ9LM0.

Wu, T. 2020. The Curse of Bigness: How Corporate Giants Came to Rule the World, London: Atlantic Books.

Index

A. Portuese, *The Battle for the Future of Antitrust*, Palgrave Studies in Institutions, Economics and Law,
https://doi.org/10.1007/978-3-031-75794-5

The manufacturer's authorised representative in the EU is Springer Nature Customer Service Centre GmbH, Europaplatz 3, 69115 Heidelberg, Germany. If you have any concerns regarding our products, please contact ProductSafety@springernature.com

Printed and bound by CPI Group (UK) Ltd, Croydon, CR0 4YY
30/09/2026
02225514-0008